THE OFFICE IDEA BOOK

Creative Solutions that Work

THE OFFICE IDEA BOOK

Creative Solutions that Work

JUDY SHEPARD

RSD PUBLISHING, INC. NEW YORK, NY

RSD Publishing, Inc.
302 Fifth Avenue
New York, NY 10001
212-279-7000
CS@rsdpublishing.com
www.rsdpublishing.com

Distributors to the trade in the United States and Canada
Innovative Logistics
575 Prospect Street
Lakewood NJ 08701
732-363-5679

Distributors outside the United States and Canada
HarperCollins International
10 East 53rd Street
New York, NY 10022-5299

Library of Congress Cataloging in Publication Data:
The Office Idea Book: Creative Solutions that Work

Printed and Bound in Hong Kong
ISBN: 978-0-9826128-9-7

CONTENTS

INTRODUCTION

In a book about office ideas one may ask, "What are these ideas? What are business leaders and designers doing to increase efficiency and productivity? In the projects showcased on these pages you will find several wide-ranging trends as well as many, more-specialized ideas. Which ones will truly contribute to profitability is for the future to tell. Yet they are design solutions in which leaders in a variety of industries believe are worth investing considerable time and resources.

The first, and biggest trend—one that affects much in its wake, and a word that you will be reading again and again—is collaboration. Companies of all shapes and sizes, from financial to creative, are eager to encourage teamwork and cooperation. This includes not just the forming of project teams, but a move toward a more comprehensive, office-wide exchange of ideas.

Facilitating collaboration are two interrelated design solutions: the open-plan office, and areas designated for group interaction. Many of the offices shown here have large, or even huge, rooms with low, or no, partitions between workstations. Sight lines reach from one end of the office to the other and coworkers sit close to one another. With these rooms comes the need for spaces in which colleagues can talk without disturbing others. Meeting rooms of many configurations, hallways wide enough for chairs and tables, lunchrooms and lounges, all provide places for people to gather, both planned and impromptu.

Transparency is another prominent idea. Closely tied to collaboration it is evidenced by the open office itself and lots of clear glass. Executives may still have private offices but they are likely to be fronted with clear glass. This trend may be a result of a move away from traditional vertical hierarchy or recent shakedowns from regulators, but it's found throughout these projects and impossible not to understand, at least in part, symbolically.

Natural light is another idea whose time has come. Windows are large and solid interior walls are few, allowing natural light to reach the center of large rooms. Atriums and skylights are in abundance, and terraces and outdoor spaces provide additional breathing room. Have leaders of the workplace finally noticed that human beings are not machines and an employee who has to go online to see if it's raining is probably not smiling?

All this natural light also reduces the need for artificial light, which leads to another big idea: being green. Water and energy conservation is everywhere. Lights in empty rooms turn off automatically, and heating and cooling systems are increasingly efficient. Materials and resources are sustainably grown and transported. These efforts are not just for LEED certification, although many projects in this book have certification, employee health and attitude are also considered important. Air quality is monitored and employees are encouraged to take green practices home.

Within these large trends there are many smaller ideas to discover. There are private nooks for employees to enjoy some alone time; there are flooring options that are easy on the feet, and acoustical solutions that are easy on the ears. There are graphics that brand the office and dining rooms that feed the hungry. There are even a slide, a hill and a ring.

THE OFFICE IDEA BOOK

Creative Solutions that Work

Acotel Group
New York, NY

Spector Group, New York, NY; Woodbury, NY

While companies in Manhattan's financial district routinely employ cutting-edge technologies, they often occupy aging buildings that require modernization. This has certainly been true for the U.S. headquarters of Acotel Group, an Italian global telecommunications company.

An evaluation of 80 Pine Street by Spector Group, designer of the one-floor, 12,000 sq. ft. facility, revealed low ceilings, awkward HVAC layouts, a profusion of pipes and other undesirable conditions. Because Acotel wanted its

workspace to portray its businesses, Spector Group envisioned a young, brainy and hip environment comprising perimeter offices and conference rooms, central open workstations, bistro, central elevator lobby and core space.

Happily, the company's desire complemented the design firm's strategies. To raise the ceiling, the design exposes the fireproof concrete structural grid and its low beams, angled sections and irregular columns, establishing an 11-foot, 9-inch, high-tech elevation with room for HVAC ducts. To

The entrance lobby sets the young and hip tone found throughout the space.

organize the chaotic core area, a "back of house wall" neatly wraps around it. To add flair, glass is used for most walls, opening stunning views to everyone, and the central space before the elevator lobby acts as an informal meeting area where all paths cross.

The result is three-dimensional, abstract, versatile and cool. When visitors pass through the bright yellow entrance portal, they know awesome things await them.

Both the bistro, above, and a conference room, below, offer stunning views of Manhattan's financial district.

The design includes central open workstations and perimeter offices.

DESIGN: **Spector Group**, New York, NY; Woodbury, NY
CLIENT: **Acotel Group,** New York, NY
PHOTOGRAPHY: **Eric Laignel**
TEXT: **Roger Yee**

Activ Financial
New York, NY

Tobin | Parnes Design, New York, NY

The reception seating area has a recessed niche displaying the company logo.

In the entry and reception area custom walnut framed barn-style doors are designed to secure and conceal the elevator doors. Shown closed, they slide outward to reveal elevator doors.

Conference room with custom glass marker board.

Activ Financial is a global market data provider serving the financial services industry. For this, their third office in New York City, and one of several worldwide, the design firm Tobin | Parnes Design was asked to transform a loft-like space—in a building formerly utilized by light manufacturing companies—into a modern, vibrant office environment.

The directive asked that the experience and character of the raw space be maintained. The high ceilings and light-filled energy of the open space were utilized to promote maximum transparency and create ease of communication within the office. The designers also needed to address the acoustical challenge of such an open space.

The reception area provides the first indication of the predominant aesthetic. Exposed concrete beams and ductwork are contrasted with a modern seating arrangement and the company's logo. The central core of the office, and the hub of activity, is an interior call center enveloped within custom acoustic ceiling panel. Carpeting and curved partitions further define the area without segregating the adjacent spaces.

Surrounding the core are perimeter offices with frameless glass fronts for maximum transparency. Natural light filters from these offices and into the office core. Interrupted only by structural columns and solid doors, the partitions between offices create a visual rhythm as one moves between the offices and workstations. There are a variety of spaces for staff to gather. A large conference room and a breakout space provide both formal and informal meeting areas and several offices contain small conference tables and casual seating areas.

Orange, a color both bold and warm and used in the Activ logo, has been integrated throughout the office. It is used to define boundaries as well as an accent in paint, wall coverings, fabric panels, upholstered furniture and artwork.

The designers at Tobin Parnes have effectively created an open, energetic office that promotes staff interaction while enhances Activ's contemporary image.

A central call center and business hub is acoustically controlled with custom acoustic ceiling panels and carpeting. Curved perimeter walls on two sides provide a sense of enclosure while leaving the call center visually connected to the adjacent spaces.

Private executive office with small conference table and casual seating area.

Private office with small conference table and custom glass marker board mounted to blue accent wall. Glass partitions allow visual connection and natural light to penetrate office core.

Support workstations, above, are visually open and naturally lit through perimeter offices. Shared breakout space, right, with casual seating.

DESIGN: **Tobin | Parnes Design**, New York, NY

CLIENT: **Activ Financial**

CONTRACTOR: **Accord Contracting & Management Corp.**

MEP ENGINEER: **TSF Engineering, P.C.**

PHOTOGRAPHY: **Vanni Archive**

Ammirati

New York, NY

CCS Architecture, New York, NY

The website of New York advertising agency Ammirati describes their work as: "Our solutions are always simple, memorable and most importantly, effective." The same could be said of the agency's new space. Designed by CCS Architecture in conjunction with Ammirati, it's restrained, with minimal decoration, but effective—a place for creative folks to devise interesting concepts and interact with each other to best advantage.

The office's Union Square location is very much in evidence through the large windows that line the long, rectangular space. Not only does light flood through the

windows, but also the invigorating atmosphere of Union Square, an area with a famous open-air market three days a week, funky restaurants and bars, and the always clogged, but endlessly interesting shopping mecca of 14th Street. This could be called the crossroads of New York City with its mixture of old-school New Yorkers, hipsters and bargain hunters. It's a stimulating location that's entirely fitting for the diverse needs of a creative agency.

Inside the office everything is open and bright. Walls and partitions are made of glass, and reflective surfaces abound. The ultra-clean and modern setting includes clear site lines

The reception area introduces visitors to the space's clean lines.

The vibrancy of Union Square is right outside the windows.

throughout the space. Although the designers created distinct work areas to facilitate team efforts and individual concentration, a sense of shared purpose prevails.

To ease the demands of long work hours, the client required the inclusion of amenities to provide the creature comforts that hard-working employees deserve. There is a well-equipped kitchen and community dining room, a ping-pong table, under-counter washer and dryer, showers and storage for bicycles—something important in an increasingly bike-friendly city.

Furnishings by USM Haller have been carefully selected to complement the overall setting and increase the feeling of spaciousness. The storage and table units provide flexibility and fulfill the storage and workspace needs of the agency, while lending their clean lines and understated elegance to the design. Innovative, magnetized glass panels allow work in progress to be displayed without disrupting the flow of open space.

Directly behind the reception area is a lounge with unhindered views of Union Square and ample amounts of natural light.

Mirrors and reflective surfaces make the space seem even more spacious than it is.

Bare, hardwood floors and white walls provide a firm base and simple lines, while furnishings by USM Haller complete the modern aesthetic—here in an executive office and a break-out room.

Almost the entire length of one side of the space is devoted to open work areas. The glass walls are magnetized allowing work to be easily displayed and rearranged.

Included in the design are amble areas for downtime. The kitchen includes a community dining table and an undercounter washer and dryer. Nearby a ping-pong table allows employees to unwind.

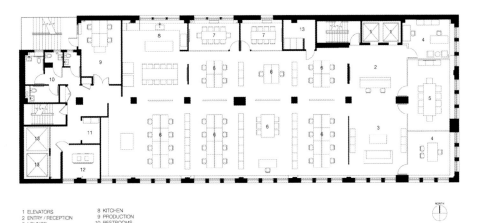

1 ELEVATORS
2 ENTRY / RECEPTION
3 LOUNGE
4 EXECUTIVE OFFICE
5 CONFERENCE ROOM
6 CREATIVE WORK BAYS
7 BREAK OUT ROOMS

8 KITCHEN
9 PRODUCTION
10 RESTROOMS
11 BICYCLE STORAGE
12 MECHANICAL ROOM
13 SERVER ROOM

NORTH

DESIGN: **CCS Architecture**, New York, NY
DESIGN PRINCIPAL: **Cass Calder Smith**
CLIENT: **Ammirati** New York, NY
PHOTOGRAPHY: **Kris Tamburello**

AOL
New York, NY

Mancini•Duffy/TSC, New York, NY

AOL's former headquarters in Dulles, VA, was a reflection of the company's previous business model of "heads-down" thinking. Workstations had limited sightlines and there was little space for collaboration. When the company recently relocated to New York City, their updated philosophy of openness and collaboration was built into the new office design.

Mancini•Duffy/TSC was tasked with the two-phase design of the three floors that AOL now occupies at 770 Broadway, a 1903 building designed by Flatiron Building architect Daniel Burnham and once home to Wanamaker's department store. Phase one encompassed floors four and five, a total of 110,000 sq. ft., and phase two took in the sixth floor and an additional 55,000 sq. ft.

Anthony P. Schirripa, FAIA, IIDA, Mancini•Duffy/TSC's Chairman and CEO and the Principal-in-Charge on the project, explains phase one: "We designed the space so that nearly every aspect reflects AOL's commitment to employee collaboration and creative teamwork. In the new space, low partitions allow open sightlines, and partitioned private offices are fewer than in the Dulles space—and glass-fronted. We took advantage of the large floor plate to create 'teaming' spaces where staff can meet to share ideas. For instance, a central corridor on each floor is designated as an 'idea gallery.' Here pin-up surfaces allow team members to display materials and share ideas."

Introduced with phase one was a component of the design that would grow in importance as the project progressed: sustainability and LEED certification. "While AOL at first wanted this project to achieve LEED Silver," Project Manager and Mancini•Duffy/TSC Senior Associate Scott Harrell says, "we were committed to helping AOL find the 'greenest' opportunities from the start so that as the project neared completion, LEED Gold was only a few steps away. As environmental awareness grew through our familiarizing our client with sustainable practices, members of the team became swept up in the process. The headquarters' LEED Gold status has also helped the space speak to its user groups, leading-edge media professionals and members of Generation Y."

Sustainable solutions include efficient HVAC systems, daylight-responsive lighting controls and water-efficient fixtures. "As the LEED architect we concentrated on the design of high-quality lighting with reduced power density, and

Phase one of the AOL design encompassed two floors of the three-floor space and reflects AOL's commitment to employee collaboration. Located on the floors are the reception area, top left, a "teaming" area, above left, and an employee café, above right. The space is clean and sophisticated with neutral finishes enlivened by punches of vibrant colors and varied textures.

In phase two of the project, attention was focused on the floor which houses the sales team. The floor has one central café/pantry that acts as a town hall of sorts—a place where everyone comes together and exchanges ideas.

The sales floor has its own reception area, above left. Branding graphics are found throughout, including a whimsical wall of characters, above right. The sales team works in an extremely collaborative atmosphere with a great degree of transparency. Workstations, below, have low partitions and private offices are glass-fronted. The designers increased the ceiling height by organizing exposed oval ductwork over workstation spines, where it also functions as a sculptural element.

In the open space of the sales floor, spaces were created to provide occasionally-needed privacy. Above are a phone room, a conference room and break-out areas.

specifying local furniture and materials with recycled content and low levels of volatile organic compounds," says Harrell. "We also worked with AOL to develop a signage and sustainability education program."

Phase two of the project involved the design of the sixth floor, where the sales team works. The floor's functionality was driven by the needs of this 300-person department engaged in the sale of online advertising. "If the previous floors were a departure from AOL's Dulles offices, the sixth floor is still more collaborative, with greater overall transparency and even lower workstations. The space is energetic and reflective of the dynamism of the group which occupies it," states Harrell.

The floor has one central café/pantry that acts as a town hall, encouraging everyone to come together and share ideas. While the fourth and fifth floors have perimeter offices with privacy glazing, here the plan is dominated by workstations. Offices are located in the interior and have clear, full-height glass for maximum visibility.

The sixth floor has a still higher percentage of recycled and green materials than the previous two, even with a tighter budget. Instead of the poured terrazzo flooring on the lower floors, cost-effective terrazzo tile was used on the sixth. It came with the added green bonus of being 70 percent recycled. Additionally, a mosaic wall was created in the pantry with glass tile of 95 percent recycled content.

The designers also had to overcome challenges created by the building itself. Schirripa explains: "In some ways 770 Broadway is an unusual building, particularly in regard to its construction, which is of highly fragile terra-cotta slabs. While concrete slabs, which are much more typical, can be trenched and then patched to accommodate electrical and data cabling, with terra cotta we found we had to core through the slab to accommodate AOL's mechanical and infrastructure requirements. This process was further complicated by the site's location above a busy department store, limiting access to the slab. We used an acoustic spray-on application to provide sound attenuation while also masking the uneven appearance of the aged building slab in areas where we chose to leave it exposed—to honor the 'bones' of the century-old building."

DESIGN: **Mancini•Duffy/TSC,** New York, NY
CLIENT: **AOL**
CONTRACTOR: **Turner Construction Company**
MEP ENGINEER: **Lizardos Engineering Associates, P.C.**
LIGHTING: **One Lux Studio**
PHOTOGRAPHY: **Adrian Wilson**

Arcturis

St. Louis, MO

Arcturis, St. Louis, MO

Arcturis, a firm specializing in architecture, interior design, landscape architecture, graphic design and workplace optimization, had outgrown their previous space. For their new office the firm selected a 30,000 sq. ft. space on the second floor of a high-rise building in the heart of downtown St. Louis. Important to the designers when concepting their own space were sustainability, flexibility, collaboration and innovation. They consider the new space to be a design test lab for experimenting with new ideas.

"Because we build our teams around the needs of our clients, the ultimate design for our own space had to be open, dynamic, flexible and functional," explains Arcturis Principal, Margaret McDonald. "Every element of the design reflects who they are while promoting their ability to serve the needs of their clients."

With sustainable design and innovation as goals, the firm's internal "Green Team" developed a LEED scorecard and other sustainable options for the space, including occupancy sensors in all conference, storage and restrooms; natural lighting throughout the studio space; and low-flow plumbing fixtures. Materials selection included only low-VOC products, recycled content, FSC certified wood and locally sourced and supplied goods. Fifty-three percent of construction waste materials were diverted from landfill, and the office is located close to public transportation. The office has received LEED-CI Silver certification.

"The space is a great tool for promoting and educating the merits of sustainable design to a variety of visitors and groups," states McDonald. "As part of Arcturis' standard sustainable best practices, the firm invites guests to participate in a 'LEED Scavenger Hunt' where sustainable innovations are tagged with graphics to help them locate and understand the many green solutions utilized throughout the space."

To promote collaboration, the office includes multiple conference rooms for presentations, learning sessions and meetings as well as open areas for interaction and socializing. Flexible furniture systems have low partitions to further encourage collaboration and allow views throughout the space. A Wii play area offers employees a place to take a break and keep the creative juices flowing. Large pin-up areas, back-lit panels and multiple flat screens communicate the firm's work to visitors.

The lobby and reception area reflects the innovative and collaborative culture at Arcturis. Back-lit panels and multiple flat screens communicate the firm's work to visitors.

Natural light and the exterior urban context are incorporated into the design, a reflection of the firm's commitment to downtown St. Louis.

IT'S A BIRD, IT'S A PLANE, IT'S A VIEW OUTSIDE!

LARGE FULL HEIGHT WINDOWS AND OPEN OFFICE WITH LOW FURNITURE HELP GIVE GREAT VIEWS TO THE OUTSIDE WHICH HAS SHOWN TO INCREASE PRODUCTIVITY

Floor-to-ceiling windows offer views of the city to more than 90 percent of the seated staff, important to a firm concerned with reducing stress and increasing productivity.

Over 60 percent of the products specified by cost are regional materials such as the bold concrete countertops in the restrooms made in St. Louis.

The space includes multiple conference and meeting rooms to support presentations, learning and meetings.

The multipurpose kitchen is combined with a hospitality meeting area.

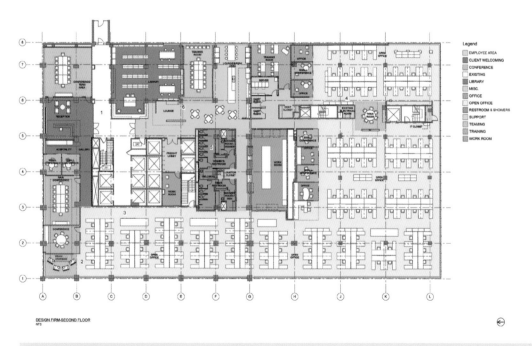

DESIGN FIRM-SECOND FLOOR
NTS

DESIGN: **Arcturis,** St. Louis, MO
CLIENT: **Arcturis,** St. Louis, MO
CONTRACTOR: **Landco Construction,** St. Louis, MO
LIGHTING: **Arcturis; William Tao & Associates,** St. Louis, MO
MEP ENGINEERING AND COMMISSIONING AGENT: **William Tao & Associates,** St. Louis, MO
PHOTOGRAPHY: **Debbie Franke,** St. Louis, MO

Astral Media
Montreal, QC, Canada

Lemay associés [architecture, design], Montreal, QC, Canada

Recently Astral Media commissioned LeMay Associes, one of the largest integrated design firms in Canada to design new office space for approximately 350 employees on four floors in the heart of the action in downtown Montreal. Among the goals for this large-scale project were elaborate new furniture standards, flexible meeting spaces, and optimizing employee interconnectivity in a contemporary, energetic and versatile working environment.

The designer's concept was inspired by key broadcasting industry words such as influence, communication, movement and exchange, based on the client's four different business segments: radio, television, advertising and digital media. Utilizing undulating and pixelated graphic elements, the designer's concept plays on the contrast between the medium and the message.

Guiding the client's transition toward a youthful and modern image, and accommodating a large number of employees previously working in various locations to a single open and standardized space proved to the be projects primary challenges.

In order to create a rhythm and gradation throughout the playful 64,583 sq. ft. facility, each floor was identified with its own color and the levels were linked by a central glass staircase. Each floor was outfitted with workstations, a main reception area, various meeting spaces including conference rooms and meeting rooms, and common service areas such as dining room, lounge, café and copy center.

Astral Media's new offices are flexible, functional and bright providing a pleasant working environment that encourages communication between employees.

Astral Media's new office provided its 350 employees, previously working in various locations, a single space to work.

The four levels are linked by a central glass staircase.

Each of the four floors has it own reception area.

The designer's concept was based on the client's four different business segments: radio, television, advertising and digital media. Utilizing undulating and pixelated graphic elements, the designer's concept plays on the contrast between the medium and the message.

In order to create a rhythm and gradation throughout the playful space each floor was identified with its own color.

The design includes workstations and various meeting spaces including conference rooms and smaller meeting rooms.

The new office includes ample space to relax and gather with colleagues.

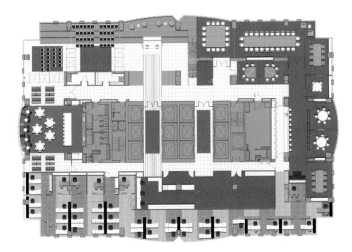

DESIGN: **Lemay associés [architecture, design]**, Montreal, QC, Canada
DESIGN TEAM: **Louis T. Lemay,** Partner in Charge; **Sandra Neill,** Associate Designer;
Chantal Ladrie, Project Manager and Designer; **Isabelle Matte,** Designer;
François Descôteaux, Designer; **Caroline Lemay,** Designer;
Marie-Élaine Globensky, Graphic Designer, **Véronique Richard,** Industrial and Graphic Designer;
Leonor Oshiro, Technician, **Phary Louis-Jean,** Technician
CLIENT: **Astral Media**
GENERAL CONTRACTOR: **Patella inc.**
ENGINEERS: **Planifitech Inc.** (electro-mechanical engineering), **Nicolet Chartrand Knoll limitée** (structural/civil engineering)
PHOTOGRAPHY: **Claude-Simon Langlois**

Ater Wynne, LLP

Portland, OR

Yost Grube Hall Architecture, Portland, OR

Ater Wynne, a law firm of 75 employees located in Portland, recently tasked Yost Grube Hall Architecture (YGH) with the design of its new 27,600 sf. ft. office.

"This doesn't look like a law firm," is a typical comment from visitors who tour Ater Wynne's new office. From the outset, Ater Wynne expressly conveyed a desire for the new office to reflect their clients, their creative approach to practice, and their vision toward the future—but avoid the appearance of a conventional law firm. Leasing the top floor of a new building in Portland's trendy Pearl District, Ater Wynne broke away from the downtown core and changed their outlook—and their view.

Inspired by the new location and its views of the Portland skyline, the design team enlarged an existing terrace and added an outdoor fireplace as a focal point for chilly evenings. They also installed sliding glass doors in the three conference rooms that adjoin the terrace, transforming the conference rooms, terrace and a gallery into a flowing event space.

It was important to Ater Wynne to include areas for meeting and socializing. In addition to the terrace and gallery, gathering spaces were created in high-traffic locations throughout the floor to encourage interaction. A vibrant lunchroom and a central library also fulfill the need for community spaces. The resulting design has many comfortable zones where colleagues and clients can informally convene.

Adding to the already abundant natural light are 28 skylights which reinforce the primary circulation. Wood floors, mahogany casework and textural stone bring warmth to the office, and the law firm's extensive art collection.

"Creating a new home for Ater Wynne was an exciting challenge," say Scott Brown, director of interior design at Yost Grube Hall Architecture. "Beyond the aesthetics and architecture, we are quite excited about the cultural and operational impact the design will have for many years ahead."

The main reception area.

Visitors stepping from the elevators into the lobby are greeted with a stunning view of the Portland skyline and the warmth of natural materials such as rich wood and natural stone.

The lobby lightwell.

In the vibrant lunchroom, bright spots of color, interesting textures and various seating options create a welcoming place for colleagues to relax.

The designers enlarged an existing terrace to take advantage of the views of downtown Portland as well as provide an informal and enticing gathering spot.

INTERIOR ARCHITECTURE & DESIGN: **Yost Grube Hall Architecture,** Portland, OR
CLIENT: **Ater Wynne**
ARCHITECTURE: **ABHT Structural Engineers**
CONTRACTOR: **Russell Construction, Inc.**
LIGHTING: **Luma Lighting Design**
PHOTOGRAPHY: **Pete Eckert, Eckert & Eckert Photography, and Jeremy Bitterman**

Bouklis Group
New York, NY

Bluarch Architecture + Interiors + Lighting
New York, NY

The Bouklis Group office in Manhattan's Financial District is the headquarters for a real estate brokerage firm. The designers at Bluarch, also of New York, were called upon to design a streamlined, open environment that would take full advantage of the 1,100 sq. ft. space.

"The design concept behind this project stems from the basic notion of horizontal separation that characterizes real estate deals and properties," explains principal Antonio Di Oronzo. "The same way plans deliver a spatial sense of real estate, or floors of a building convey the layering of a property, or stacking conveys the aggregation of masses based on zoning regulations, we wanted to clearly define the project with color, materials, and lighting… horizontally."

The first horizontal layer—a layer of blue—is created with the desks and carpet. In a perfectly matching shade of blue, the workstations and carpet form a fluid line that adds a sense of movement to the space. The continuous blue layer also somewhat hides the boundary between floor and desk and makes the space seem larger then it actually is.

The next layer is composed of a system of wood dividers that provide the needed amount of privacy for each salesperson. These elements also contain the computer monitors and the laser-cut company logo. Glass partitions offer further separation where needed while preserving the continuity of the design. Above all is a layer of white consisting of the ceiling and lighting.

The three layers of the design—blue, natural wood and white—give a sense of fluidity to the Bouklis office.

Glass partitions allow private offices to remain connected to the layered design.

DESIGN: **Bluarch Architecture + Interiors + Lighting,** New York, NY
CLIENT: **Tom Bouklis**
PHOTOGRAPHY: **Oleg March**

Bryan Cave LLP
Irvine, CA

AREA Architecture, Los Angeles, CA

The reception area sets the casual, yet serious tone of the office. Staircase is to the rear and the boardroom is to the right.

Bryan Cave LLP, a law firm based in St. Louis, Missouri, recently relocated their Newport Beach, California, office to a newly constructed high-rise building in Irvine, California. AREA Architecture was challenged to develop a new concept for the 41,000 sq. ft. space which would position the law firm as a leader in their new community, and complement the area. "There is a graciousness of doing business in Orange County that is expressed in our architectural design and selection of finishes and furnishings," says Henry Goldston of AREA Architecture.

The goal of the project was to create a casual, yet serious and sophisticated atmosphere with open areas to promote camaraderie and allow the firm's 125 employees to enjoy the stunning views. The architects located the main public conference rooms on two floors at the reception area and staircase. The library, employee lounge and additional conference rooms are located in the corners of the building,

ensuring natural light and open spaces for gatherings and relaxed interaction.

Although finishes have a sense of elegance and richness, the designers were always careful to be cost effective. Carefully placed exotic and reforested veneers of clustered English Sycamore, Hawaiian Koa, English Brown Oak and East Indian Laurel are combined with chiseled planes of coated drywall and accents of French St. Laurent marble. Promoting energy conservation and sustainability are renewable bamboo flooring and the extensive use of clere-story glass to open the space and allow ample amounts of natural light. Pinpoint LED lights give definition to the stair.

To withstand the large number of both internal and client related meetings, conference tables are a combination of recycled engineered stone and natural granite. State of the art audiovisual equipment provides easy communication to other offices and clients.

The interior connecting stair is highlighted with pinpoint LED lights.

Cuyahoga Community College ®

Due Date

Apr 23

Thank you for visiting the Tri-C Libraries!

Hours
Monday — Thursday
8 a.m. — 8 p.m.

Friday — Saturday
9 a.m. — 2 p.m.

Sunday
Closed

The l
video t
remo

Manage Your Library
Account Online
www.tri-c.edu/library

The assistant workstations are given privacy with green-hued sheets of glass that sit above custom veneered millwork.

A conference room is located at the top of the interconnecting stair. The elegance and richness of the design complement the graciousness of Orange County.

Located in the corners of the building are a open conference and interactive corner, top, and a casual conference area, above. Both provide light-drenched spaces for colleagues to gather.

DESIGN: **AREA Architecture,** Los Angeles, CA
CLIENT: **Bryan Cave LLP**
CONTRACTOR: **Clune Construction Company**
LIGHTING: **Penumbra Architectural Illumination**
PHOTOGRAPHY: **Benny Chan/Fotoworks**

Bureau 100

Montreal, QC, Canada

NFOE et associés architectes, Montreal, QC, Canada

The project's aesthetic approach utilizes a subtle play between verticals and horizontals.

NFOE et associés architectes, founded in 1912, recently moved its offices to Old Montreal into the city's first sky-scraper—better known as the New York Life Building. NFOE's Bureau 100 facing the historic Place d'Armes square, is therefore integrated with an environment that evokes the history of the firm founded by Ernest I. Barott.

A successful relationship with the owner resulted in a large-scale restoration project on the first two floors, occupied by NFOE. The interior, which had deteriorated considerably, was returned to its original state, with impressive Corinthian columns, ornate ceiling moldings, and original woodwork. All of this, plus the immense windows and light colors, contribute to creating a stimulating work environment.

The project's aesthetic approach links the past and present. Partitions from previous renovations on both floors have been removed. Into a space rich in architectural details, the simple, elegant furnishings are utilized. The open-plan space workstations encourage interaction among groups, while offering the opportunity for individual thought and reflection. Zones for improvised meetings are located in proximity to the workstations. The levels are composed of open spaces that emphasize the original ornamentations of the columns, ceilings, moldings, and woodwork. The bank vault is still in place on the ground floor and is now used as a library.

Each floor has its own distinct ambience: the ground floor is grandiose, whereas the upper floor is intimate. The ceilings featured exposed infrastructure with the ornamentations. The ground floor has a high ceiling with large windows offering stunning views and is bathed in natural light, which is diffused into the workspace by the light color of the walls and furniture. Dark accents on the walls add depth. The second floor has a lower ceiling, lending intimacy to the work areas. A series of superimposed drop ceilings amplifies the height reduction and acts as a series of horizontal slabs contrasting with the vertical columns.

The original woodwork and fireplace have been preserved in the ground-floor conference room. Above the woodwork, the dark-colored walls amplify the height under the ceiling and visually detach the ornate moldings from the wall. The contemporary lighting fixtures appear to fall, like water drops, from the ceiling. The partners' offices are at one end overlooking Place d'Armes where visual permeability is kept with the use of glass panels as partitions and doors. At the back, upstairs is the conference room with large window and semi-circular woodwork and a lighting fixture echoing the shape of the window.

Simple, elegant furnishings are utilized within a space rich in architectural details.

The ground floor is bathed in natural light and has a high ceiling with large windows offering stunning views.

The second floor has a lower ceiling, lending intimacy to the work areas. A series of superimposed drop ceilings amplifies the height reduction and acts as a series of horizontal slabs contrasting with the vertical columns.

The original woodwork has been preserved in the ground-floor conference room. Above the woodwork, the dark-colored walls amplify the height under the ceiling and visually detach the ornate moldings from the wall.

DESIGN: **NFOE et associés architectes**, Montreal, QC, Canada
PROJECT MANAGER: **Masa Fukushima, Rafie Sossanpour**
DESIGN TEAM: **NFOE team**
CLIENT: **NFOE et associés architectes**
CONTRACTOR: **BTL Construction**
LIGHTING DESIGN: **NFOE team**
PHOTOGRAPHY: **Stéphane Brügger**

Cendes
Chengdu, China

Cendes, Chengdu, China

The new Chengdu headquarters of Cendes architecture is located on the second and third floors of an apartment building and comprises a mix of common areas, open-plan work areas and private offices. There is space for visitors to relax, an exhibition space, spacious conference rooms, and open stairwells offering views of multiple floors.

The company has operated in China for more than ten years and, in addition to Chengdu, has offices in Beijing, Shanghai and Xi'am. The new space in Chengdu houses a staff of almost 400 that includes architects, engineers, landscape and interior designers, graphic designers, 3D digital artists and administrative personnel. Heidi Meng of Cendes says, "The collaborative nature of the design-related professions called for an open space concept. The main purpose of this concept is to create an environment conducive to people in various design disciplines working together—helping to improve team spirit and collaboration."

When designing their own office, the team at Cendes took full advantage of every square foot of the 39,826 sq. ft. (3,700 sq. meter) space. The floor plan is U-shaped with the longest axis running north/south and shorter, east/west wings enclosing the building's quiet, inner courtyard. The reception area, gallery and spacious conference rooms are located in the northern east/west wing and entered from the courtyard. Once past reception, a single unifying circulation runs through the rest of the office. Facing the street are generous open-plan offices that house the various design teams and facing the courtyard are private offices and team meeting rooms. In the southern east/west wing is a multi-level open space and open stairwell.

The materials utilized—concrete, polished wood, steel and glass—provide a refined look and unify the diverse spaces.

Visitors to Cendes architecture are met with an elegant reception area and gallery. Materials of steel, stone, glass and wood create a unifying aesthetic throughout the office. To facilitate collaboration, design teams are located in large, open areas.

DESIGN/CLIENT: **Cendes**, Chengdu, China
DESIGNER: **Andrew Chen**
LIGHTING: **PAK CORPORATION**
PHOTOGRAPHY: **Nicolas Marino**

Christner Inc.

St. Louis, MO

Christner Inc., St. Louis, MO

Christner Inc, a firm offering architectural, interior and graphic design, as well as landscape architecture and urban design, recently relocated to the top floor of a 1980s office building in St. Louis. In business for 50 years, the firm is known for design excellence, innovative methods and sustainable solutions. These skills and abilities were put to good use for the planning and designing of their own new office.

The move permitted the firm to bring all of its 60 employees together on one level, and eliminate duplication of resources. The new design encourages communication and collaboration—important to the firm's multi-disciplinary and highly collaborative practice model. Also important to the project was cost effectiveness and the achievement of sustainable design.

The building features a compact floor plate and large ribbon windows that allow in natural light and offer expansive views of the St. Louis skyline, including the city's famous Arch. "The office was envisioned as a design workshop," says Christner's Dan Jay. "The zoning of 'solid' and 'open' spaces creates clear-view corridors that link principal spaces and allow light to penetrate deep into the space."

Workstations are table-based, with low dividers to allow easy communication and maximize access to daylight. A full 96 percent of the workspaces have direct window views. Although conference rooms and four offices are enclosed to provide acoustical privacy, glass partitions and doors ensure transparency.

The central reception space serves as the hub of the office. Adjacent to the reception area is the Design Review Studio—a collaborative meeting and work space which can be opened to the lobby for events and social functions or closed with floor-to-ceiling glass for client meetings. Vibrant and contrasting colors, wood, and variations in floor finishes reinforce the organizational and spatial richness of the office.

In the entrance lobby and primary public spaces, the existing concrete floor was simply ground and polished, eliminating the energy consumption associated with installing new flooring materials. Other sustainable practices include occupancy sensor controlled lighting, a paperless initiative and the reduction of paper storage capacity by 50 percent from the former office. Materials with low Volatile Organic Compounds (VOC) were also selected. The office was recently awarded LEED-CI Gold certification.

The lobby and reception area is the hub of the office. The Design Review Studio opens to the reception area and the spaces can be combined for all-office meetings and social functions.

Glass partitions from Dirtt have very high acoustic properties and can be moved or reinstalled, contributing to Christner's sustainability goals.

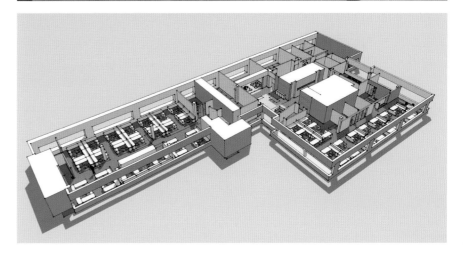

Low-height, reconfiguarble components from Knoll—the "big table" model—create spaces that are inherently collaborative. The same system is used in workstations, offices and training rooms to carry through the clean lines, elegant style. The components also provide the ability to plug in multiple gadgets.

Communication and collaboration are important to the firm's multi-disciplinary and highly collaborative practice model. The relocation allowed Christner to bring all of its employees onto one, 15,000 sq. ft. level.

Textured wood paneling—100 percent recycled elm from a dismantled dairy barn— in the lobby and elevator core was selected to provide a counterpoint to the mostly bright, hard surfaces.

N ⊕

1. Reception	7. Office	13. Kitchen
2. Support	8. Admin	14. Interiors Library
3. Design Library	9. Conference Room	15. Accounting
4. Design Review Studio	10. Training/Conference	16. IT
5. North Studio	11. Meeting	17. Storage
6. West Studio	12. Print Room	18. Marketing

DESIGN: **Christner Inc.,** St. Louis, MO
CLIENT: **Christner Inc.**
CONTRACTOR: **ISC Contracting,** St. Louis, MO
PHOTOGRAPHY: **Christner Inc.**

Edward Jones Training Facility

St. Louis, MO

Arcturis, St. Louis, MO

Edward Jones is a financial investment firm that serves nearly seven million investors in North America. At the core of the firm's approach is the relationship established between financial advisor and client—a relationship that starts with a face-to-face meeting. The firm invests much time and energy in training its associates and in attracting new talent to the company. The new 380,000 sq. ft. training facility, designed by Arcturis, is a testament to Edward Jones' investment in its people. The goal of the designers was to create a building that supports the investment firm's culture of "connection, collaboration and inspiration."

The building can accommodate more than 1,400 people for training and, in addition, has office space for more than 700 associates. It includes training rooms, role-playing rooms, various classroom configurations, conference rooms, cafeteria, a pre-function area, a 600-seat multipurpose room and offices.

A four-story atrium and pre-function space welcomes new associates for training. The area also works as a central organizational spine with the main program spaces branching to either side. The four floors surrounding the atrium are dedicated to training and are connected with a "communicat-

The building's north-south orientation was conceived to maximize energy efficiency and allow an abundance of natural light into the building. An exterior courtyard, adjacent to the pre-function space, can be used for various corporate events.

The building's pre-function space is used for various events. Exterior materials include terra cotta, zinc and limestone, and custom pendant light fixtures create a visual rhythm.

Words that describe the firm's values and culture are displayed on the terra cotta wall in the pre-function space.

The facility provides various classroom configurations, above left, equipped with AV systems to support technology needs. A variety of open and closed meeting and lounge spaces, above right, were designed to support the different levels and phases of training.

ing bridge." The bridge allows associates to easily navigate the open space and find small, informal opportunities to interact. Forty training rooms form the basic grid of the building and present an efficient layout for the workstations on the five upper office floors.

A large multipurpose room can be divided into a number of configurations to allow the greatest degree of flexibility for both training and business presentations. At full capacity it seats 600 people. Also included is a large full-service cafeteria that can serve more than 500 people and a dining area that overlooks an inviting exterior courtyard.

"A key design goal was to develop a transparent feel to the building, bringing the outside in and highlighting the movement of people inside. The effective arrangement of gathering spaces—the main entry, the four-story atrium with connector bridges acting as break areas, an open stair, the pre-function space, and dining area overlooking an exterior courtyard—all create inspiring, light-filled spaces for people to connect, collaborate and learn," states Arcturis Principal, Margaret McDonald.

A communication stair, above left, connects the first through third floors and skylights allow light to pour into the space. The bridge connecting the wings of the building, above right, is both an important circulation space and a communication hub. On it are located convenient spaces for those in training to relax and continue the learning process outside the training room.

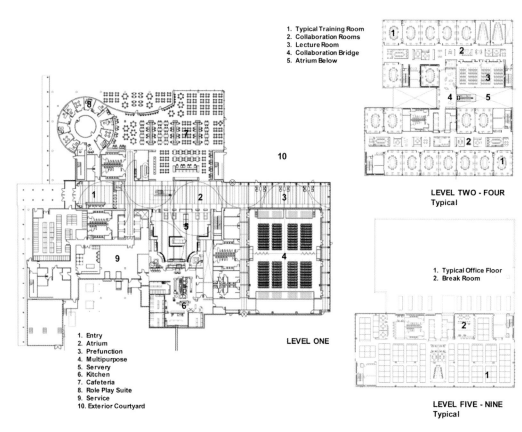

1. Typical Training Room
2. Collaboration Rooms
3. Lecture Room
4. Collaboration Bridge
5. Atrium Below

LEVEL TWO - FOUR
Typical

1. Typical Office Floor
2. Break Room

LEVEL FIVE - NINE
Typical

1. Entry
2. Atrium
3. Prefunction
4. Multipurpose
5. Servery
6. Kitchen
7. Cafeteria
8. Role Play Suite
9. Service
10. Exterior Courtyard

LEVEL ONE

The multipurpose room, above left, can be divided into smaller rooms to meet simultaneous meeting requirements. In the kitchen, above right, reflective materials are combined with glass wall tiles and stainless steel equipment. Orange is used as an accent color to recall the terra cotta wall in the pre-function space. Horizontal light bars are suspended above the food stations and reinforced with horizontal signage.

The dining area offers a variety of seating arrangements and a connection to the exterior courtyard and outdoor dining.

DESIGN: **Arcturis,** St. Louis, MO
CLIENT: **Edward Jones**
CONTRACTOR: **McCarthy,** St. Louis, MO
MEP/FP ENGINEER: **Henneman Engineering,** St. Louis, MO
STRUCTURAL ENGINEER: **Alper Audi,** St. Louis, MO
CIVIL ENGINEER: **Jacobs,** St. Louis, MO
AV/ACOUSTICAL: **Waveguide,** Atlanta, GA
PHOTOGRAPHY: **Dave Burk, Hedrich Blessing Photographers,** Chicago, IL

Foley & Lardner LLP
Los Angeles, CA

AREA Architecture, Los Angeles, CA

Visitors to the new downtown Los Angeles offices of Foley & Lardner proceed from the elevator lobby, left, to the dramatic reception desk and staircase, above.

Foley & Lardner LLP, a law firm headquartered in Milwaukee, WI, had long maintained an office in Century City, on the Westside of Los Angeles. With the recent resurgence of downtown Los Angeles—the center of all things cool and hip—as the prime location for major law firms in the city, it was decided to make a move to the area. A space of 62,000 sq. ft. in a prominent high-rise building was secured for the firm's 160 employees.

The law firm turned to AREA Architecture to create a new, image-enhancing office. It was vital that an identity for Foley

& Lardner be created that would set them apart from their competition and position them as a serious player, but one with a more casual atmosphere.

"Curves and angles create excitement and give a rectilinear building a hip but classic sense of style." That was the mantra given to the architects by Deborah Wasson of Foley & Lardner, with whom the architects have worked for 15 years. To meet the challenge posed by the rectilinear building the architects carved light coves, stairs and ceiling elements from drywall, often with flowing curves, but without sacrificing timeless design. "Knowing your client well gives a sense of free expression that is sometimes more difficult to achieve with a new relationship," says AREA's Walt Thomas.

That sense of expression is introduced to visitors at the reception area with its dramatically curving ceiling, desk and floor pattern. Contrasting these curves are the angles of the staircase directly behind the desk. Enclosed in economical filmed glass, the stairs allow light from the windows beyond to flood the space. Upscale multi-purpose rooms, divisible with ceiling mounted partitions, and other state of the art audiovisual conference rooms create a public hub that bustles with activity and interaction.

Energy conservation and environment issues were met without creating budgetary obstacles. LED lights are used as a decorative random star pattern over the stair and reception area, as well as more functional purposes throughout the space. Separate perimeter lighting and HVAC controls also minimizes energy consumption. Exotic veneers such as European Walnut Burl and Indonesian oak were carefully selected from renewable sources. Even the artwork collection was recycled from a former space and refurbished to appear new.

Corridor, stairs and break-out area all display the classic angles and graceful curves that define the design and dispel the challenge presented by the rectilinear building.

A multipurpose room, above, incorporates ceiling mounted partitions. The open assistant area, below, uses filmed glass that lets in natural light without sacrificing privacy.

DESIGN: **AREA Architecture,** Los Angeles, CA
CLIENT: **Foley & Lardner LLP**
CONTRACTOR: **Howard Building Corporation**
LIGHTING: **Penumbra Architectural Illumination**
PHOTOGRAPHY: **Benny Chan/Fotoworks**

Forest Solutions Group

New York, NY

Spector Group, New York, NY; Woodbury, NY

Visitors are introduced to the futuristic space in the reception waiting area.

How can a physical environment support an organization's brands? Consider Forrest Solutions Group's recent introduction of two revamped business units, FSS for enterprise-wide staffing solutions and FSO for on-site outsourcing, the latest developments from a successful business founded in 1976 by CEO Mitchell D. Weiner.

The company's new, one-floor, 20,000 sq. ft. Manhattan headquarters, designed by Spector Group, impresses employees and visitors alike with its futuristic, all-white space and versatile accommodations for FSS and FSO. Comprising a reception area, private offices, boardroom, conference rooms, hotelling offices and communications center, the facility celebrates the power of teamwork by enhancing the capabilities of clients, prospects and candidates as well as the company's own employees. Accordingly, many key facilities and amenities directly promote interaction, communication and movement, such as the illuminated glass partitions that integrate company rebranding logos, slogans and colors through laminated interlayers, state-of-the-art meeting facilities (witness the "Imaginarium" or boardroom, for example), energy-efficient power and lighting systems (following sustainable green design principles), edgy yet comfortable contemporary furniture, renewable building materials (including glass, porcelain tile, carpet, paint and certified wood) and state-of-the-art technology and equipment. In assessing the new space, Weiner concludes, "Spector Group delivered on our every need, on time and within budget."

The company refers to their boardroom as an "Imaginarium."

The gleaming white interior is accented with spots of color, selectively placed. Open workstations, below, receive an abundance of natural light.

The CEO office, top, facilitates multiple meetings and communication and teamwork are further promoted in such areas as the "Think Tank," above left and "Fish Bowl" conference rooms, above right.

DESIGN: **Spector Group**, New York, NY; Woodbury, NY
CLIENT: **Forest Solutions,** New York, NY
PHOTOGRAPHY: **Eric Laignel**
TEXT: **Roger Yee**

Gummo
Amsterdam, The Netherlands

i29 interior architects, Amsterdam, The Netherlands

Gummo, an advertising agency in Amsterdam, was going to be occupying a space in an old newspaper building for only two years. Both the agency and their design firm, i29 interior architects, also of Amsterdam, agreed that this was the perfect opportunity to practice extreme moderation in design and furnishing solutions. The mantra for the project was "reduce, reuse, recycle," and it was *not* an empty slogan.

The designers at i29 took their design cues from Gummo's design philosophy, "simple, uncomplicated, no-nonsense, yet unquestionably stylish with a twist of humor." Starting with a wide, open space, they identified the various sections of the office layout by painting large blocks on the floor—white and gray.

Then the fun began. The designers collected a few vans full of furnishings from local charity and second-hand shops, Marktplaats (the Dutch eBay) and whatever was left over from the old office, and gave everything a spraying of gray, environmentally-safe paint. Then all of the furnishings were carefully placed on the pre-painted floor, creating clearly defined islands of work spaces.

The results did minimal damage to the client's wallet and provided a stylish and fun-filled space for the creative folks at Gummo—a case study in environmental friendliness and cost-effectiveness.

Every item in the temporary office, including a bust of Jesus, was spray painted with polyurea Hotspray—an environmentally-friendly paint—in a unifying shade of gray.

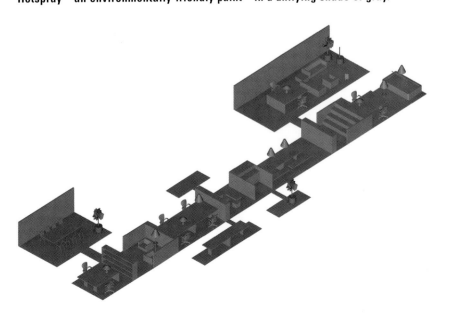

Different areas of the office are defined with paint on the floor, creating spaces for work and recreation. All of the furniture was second-hand.

DESIGN: **i29 interior architects**, Amsterdam, The Netherlands
CONTRACTOR: **Stefan Klopper**
COATING: **Krimpex Coating systems (hotspray)**
CLIENT: **Gummo,** Amsterdam, The Netherlands
PHOTOGRAPHY: **i29 interior architects**

Hewlett Packard (HP)

Plano, TX

Michael Malone Architects, Inc. Dallas, TX

EDS, recently acquired by Hewlett Packard, is a computer services company that designs, installs, maintains and operates technology systems throughout the world for all aspects of global business and government.

For many people, including potential clients, technology services are hard to define and understand so EDS (now HP) asked Michael Malone Architects to create an environment—a Marketplace—to present their capabilities to a diverse group of decision makers. The customers need to be provided not only with an understanding of the technology offerings, but be able to sample the corporate culture of HP while being shown the hospitality suitable to guests in the facility.

"HP wanted to convey that they were a stable and capable provider of technology services and that they were innovators and thought leaders," explains principal Michael Malone. "It was our specific task to create an environment that was a three dimensional manifestation of their corporate culture and reinforce that message with architecture in every possible way."

The center breaks down the visitor experience into three components: First, the lobby and a coffee bar provide spaces for greeting and hospitality. These areas are bright, inviting and comfortable. Second, presentations are made in the demonstration and exhibit spaces, including hands-on applications of the technology and services. The third component is the meeting and collaboration environment with its elaborately appointed conference rooms and supporting access for dining and breakout sessions.

To convey the message that technology enhances daily life and commerce, it is integrated into the spaces and exhibits, making it part of the message, not the message's primary focus. "The goal is to help customers and guests understand that this technology is there to support their efforts, not an end in itself," says Malone.

"While the look of the space supports the idea that this company is at the cutting edge of technology," continues Malone, "it is also warm and accessible. The design strives to use materials that are appropriate to the support of the messages and not call undue attention to them. For that reason a neutral color and finish pallet was selected, allowing the exhibits and graphics to take center stage."

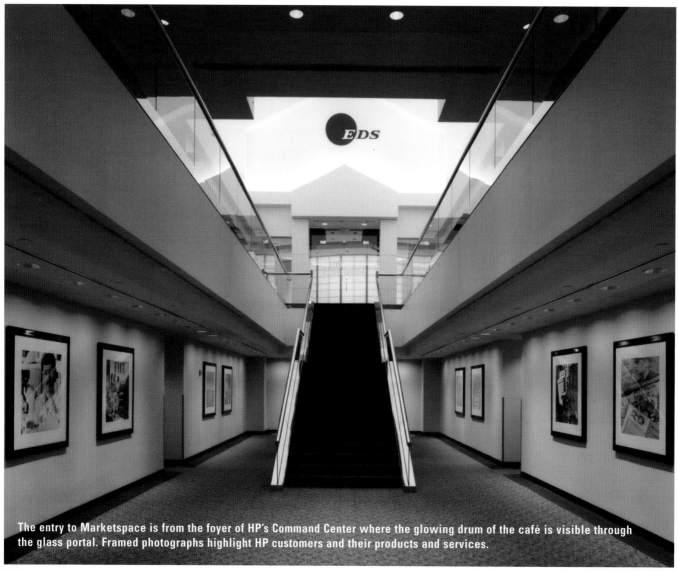

The entry to Marketspace is from the foyer of HP's Command Center where the glowing drum of the café is visible through the glass portal. Framed photographs highlight HP customers and their products and services.

Entry lobby features a glowing cylindrical wall, at right in the photo, surrounding the café. Applied to the wall are the names of HP clients from around the world.

The reception desk with monitor that can be programmed to greet visitors, above left. Entry to the café is immediately beyond the desk. A typical access corridor, above right, to the back of the house areas on display. The technology required to support the exhibits and demonstrations is an integral part of the Marketspace experience.

View of the café with web surfing stations and table that can be reconfigured for various sized groups. The door beyond (shown opened below and closed at left) provides access to the overlook to the Command Center.

The café at the Marketspace with coffee bar demonstrating Mr. Java. The espresso machine uses a memory chip in the cup to make the user's exact coffee drink every time the cup is placed in the dispenser. This space is used for breakout, informal presentations, web surfing and technology demonstrations.

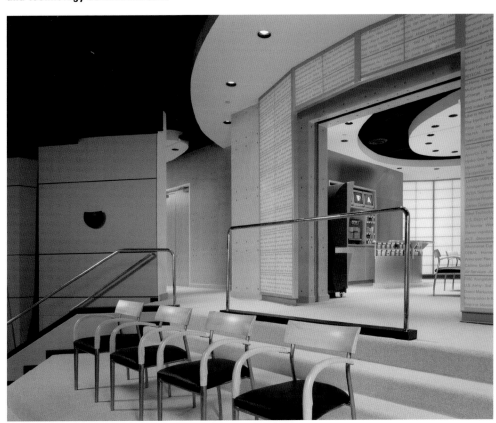

The Command Center can be viewed from Marketspace and is accessed from the café. The doors open to allow access and the view is a highlight of any tour.

The demonstration area is a ring of monitors and computer controlled exhibits that illustrate various services available to HP customers. The informal layout allows for viewing at a pace that suits the visitors and allows for additional exploration and demonstration as questions arise.

Collaboration rooms provide HP, and their customer's, places to share their capabilities and needs and define the technologies needed to support their enterprises. The round table supports various technologies and is centered below a ceiling cloud that focuses light on participants in discussions.

Visitors to Marketspace overlook the Command Center where HP's worldwide networks are monitored and managed.

DESIGN: **Michael Malone Architects, Inc.,** Dallas, TX
Michael Malone, AIA, Principal
Talmadge Smith, AIA, Project Manager
Rob Romero, AIA
Shani Dixon
CLIENT: **EDS**
GRAPHICS AND BRANDING: **Pentagram**
CONTRACTOR: **Structuretone**
LIGHTING: **Michael Malone Architects, Inc.**
EXHIBIT FABRICATORS: **Creations at Dallas**
PHOTOGRAPHY: **Jud Haggard Photography**

Highland Capital Management

Dallas, TX

Michael Malone Architects, Inc. Dallas, TX

The reception area is a celebration of maple. It is used in the floors, wall paneling and ceilings, and forms a backdrop for the art by Janet McGreal. This sustainable hardwood, harvested from the client's own forests was selected for its light coloring and ability to reflect light. The free form reception desk welcomes visitors and guests and establishes the tone of Highland Capital management as a progressive, forward looking firm. A ceiling cloud defines the seating area nested on a custom leather edged rug.

Open office furniture is clustered in groups of four and arranged beneath a wood and aluminum ceiling cloud. Glass block encloses an end cap conference room.

Highland Capital Management is a diversified financial services company and a large and experienced alternative credit manager. Their investors are public pension plans, foundations and endowments, corporations, financial institutions, governments, and high net worth individuals. Highland Capital Management invests for investors in hedge funds, long-only commingled funds, separate accounts, private equity, and collateralized loan obligations.

Michael Malone Architects was challenged to design a new office for Highland Capital that was open, cutting-edge and conducive to collaboration. The goal was to create an environment that would both reflect the company's dedication to progressive ideas and act as a tool to allow the forward-thinking staff to excel at the business of managing and investing money.

"Literal and implied transparency was the most important element of the design for the company," says principal Michael Malone. "In the wake of the financial crisis, they felt it was important to create an office environment that was open, collaborative and encouraged interaction between teams. Virtually all of the work takes place in open office environments, supplanted by closed conference rooms when privacy is necessary. Even the partner offices are all glass

with large sliding walls that open to their teams who are located close by."

For the open office environment, the designers developed a basic planning module around a single group of workstations arranged in a cruciform. The concept—"benching"— allows the resulting team to be closely connected, while providing a way for the ubiquitous technology and computer equipment to be accommodated with minimal clutter to the work surface. The modules, or groupings, are arranged in rows throughout the open floors and further defined by wood and metal ceiling features the designers call clouds. Placed above each module, the clouds support both direct and indirect lighting. From their workstations employees also have unobstructed access to windows and exterior views.

According to Malone the most dramatic aspect of the design was the use of maple as a thematic element. "Maple is a sustainable hardwood and here became the main signature element used in furniture, paneling, ceilings and other prominent design features. Highland was heavily invested in sustainable hardwood forests and a decision was made early to use light wood, not typical for financial companies, to open up the space and maximize reflected light."

With a few exceptions all staff sits at open office stations. When acoustic privacy is required glass walled conference rooms provide places for meetings and conference calls. Dark carpet contrasts with the white laminate, aluminum and maple of the systems furniture.

Typical team accommodations at Highland Capital group four workstations in a cruciform pattern under a wood and aluminum ceiling cloud. Technology and monitors are suspended from the center of the "bench" and allow a clear work surface area and some privacy.

The chairman's suite, above, is a design primer for the whole project. In this space, all of the visual elements used elsewhere are part of the larger composition. A custom desk follows the curve of the ceiling cloud and is matched by its twin, the conference table beyond the dividing wall of glass. This table allows meetings to continue when the chairman receives a call and has to step out briefly. A cluster of stations for support staff is placed outside the entry to the chairman's suite, below. A glass and maple paneled wall provides acoustic privacy for the suite.

The main boardroom is a crisp and warm wood paneled space featuring a continuous cantilevered credenza with marble tops. The ceiling has a white cloud floating in the wood border. The wide plank floors are maple and the inlaid maple table was custom designed and manufactured for the space. The windows provide dramatic views of downtown Dallas and the art is by Shane Pennington.

Conference rooms, above left, have been created at the end cap of each of the building's elevator cores. The rooms feature custom inlaid maple tables in the shape of the room itself. Glass block allows in natural light, while providing visual privacy. Smaller conference rooms, above right, are accorded the same level of finish and detail as the larger rooms. The curving walls soften the space and focus attention on the custom table shaped to highlight the intimacy of this warmly paneled room.

Partner offices use maple and aluminum finishes and feature marble-topped work surfaces. Supporting the transparency theme of the office design, the walls slide open to allow partners to have full access to their teams beyond. Adjacent to each partner office is a glass walled conference room.

At the end of each floor glass walled conference rooms are clustered to provide places for private meetings, above. The glass block walls of the end cap conference rooms are beyond. Crisp new restrooms, below, both luminous and bright, were a client request. Large format porcelain tiles clad the walls and English slate covers the floors. Laminated glass stall doors provide borrowed light to the rest of the room.

Meals are provided to all staff at Highland Capital Management, making the break room very important to the design and organization of the space. The large center counter permits food deliveries to be arranged for pickup by staff, and surrounding cabinets provide access to snacks, beverages and condiments. Utilitarian, but well appointed, the break room is finished in black and white solid surface materials. Banquettes allow for quick lunch breaks within the space itself.

DESIGN: **Michael Malone Architects, Inc.**, Dallas, TX
Michael Malone, AIA, Principal
Audrey Maxwell, Associate AIA, Project Manager
Paul Pascarelli, AIA
Livia Franca, International AIA
Peter Fetzer
CLIENT: **Highland Capital Management**
MEP CONSULTANTS: **Schmidt & Stacy**
STRUCTURAL ENGINEER: **Stenstrom Schneider, Inc.**
CONTRACTOR: **Highland Builders, Inc.**
LIGHTING: **Michael Malone Architects, Inc.**
ART CONSULTANTS: **Emil and Gianna Cerullo**
ARCHITECTURAL WOODWORK: **Solid Details**
SYSTEMS AND OFFICE FURNITURE: **G L Seaman and Knoll**
CUSTOM CONFERENCE TABLES: **Fetzer, Inc.**
PHOTOGRAPHY: **Jud Haggard Photography**

Holiday Films Production Studio

Toronto, ON, Canada

Altius Architecture Inc., Toronto, ON, Canada

Holiday Films Production Studio is a 3,000 sq. ft. commercial office and production studio located in the Eclipse Whitewear Building in Toronto. In renovating the space, Altius Architecture Inc., also of Toronto, was careful to preserve the historic integrity of the four-story building, built in 1903 and listed as a Toronto Heritage property.

Important to the client was that their company's philosophy, culture and image be carefully considered in the selection of colors, materials and finishes. Altius also took ergonomic standards and health and safety into account.

"The office is considered a basement space since it is located four feet underground and houses some of the building's mechanical systems servicing the four stories above," explains Michele Bertussi of Altius. "This type of space is challenging, as you have to work around the existing ductwork and systems while overcoming basement gloominess by strategically selecting colors, materials and lighting."

The renovation included combining two existing office spaces into one open concept production studio with four private offices, one large boardroom, a directors' lounge/reception area, espresso bar and kitchen. The boardroom is the center of the plan. It is a "box" enclosed in laminated milk glass, around which circulation flows 360 degrees. Adjacent to the boardroom is the directors' lounge that doubles as the reception area—a place where people congregate for casual meetings, parties and brainstorming sessions.

The open studio is a space where producers and support crew come and go depending on the job in production. It is multifunctional and can support the needs of a few or many. The resulting space is inviting, contemporary and functional.

The directors' lounge/reception area features a stunning walnut wall.

Circulation in the open studio flows around the milk-glass enclosed conference room.

Located four feet underground, the office's windows give an unusual perspective of the vibrant street scene, something of a movie set in and of itself. The directors lounge/reception area, right, is an inviting space where people congregate for casual meetings, parties or brainstorming sessions. Iconic furniture pieces, including the Barcelona chairs and Fat Alberts lamps, give the space a timeless quirky quality.

The multi-functional open studio, above, includes red acoustic wall panels mounted to the table tops—providing privacy, a place to tack notes and sound absorption. The center of the design is the boardroom, below, enclosed in milk glass and sporting Holiday Film's signature red color. Task lighting is suspended from a recessed red box, and an input module for smart technology is recessed into the Douglas Fir table. The red carpet tile helps to differentiate the boardroom from its surroundings.

A simple, clean office, above left, and the kitchen, above right. The designers added a water pump to bring water to the otherwise dry kitchen and installed the Blanco Linus single-handle faucet, white quartz counter-tops and red back-painted glass backsplash. The high-gloss, highly-reflective cabinets are in keeping with the entire space, where light bounces freely.

DESIGN: **Altius Architecture Inc.**, Toronto, ON, Canada
CLIENT: **Holiday Films**
PHOTOGRAPHY: **Emily Nieves**

Innocent
London, UK

Stiff + Trevillion Architects, London, UK

When Innocent, makers of fruit juices and smoothies, asked Stiff + Trevillion to design their new offices, they wanted a space that reflected the ethos and nature of their company. A quirky, unusual organization with youth and energy to spare, they needed space and they wanted to be different.

Innocent has been different since their founding in 1999. While selling smoothies at a music festival, the soon-to-be founders of the company put up a big sign asking people if they thought the juice makers should give up their day jobs and start their own company. People voted with their empty cups—throwing them in either a "yes" or "no" bin. By the end of the weekend the "yes" bin was running over, so Innocent was born.

With such a start, it's not surprising to learn the following from Stiff + Trevillion's Rebecca Snow: "All aspects of this project turned all traditional concepts of the 'office' on their heads. It proved unequivocally that an office does not need to be constrained, orthodox and regimented. It offered a totally new way of looking at working life, embracing fun,

creativity, dynamism and freshness, overthrowing the normal expectations."

Innocent needed a large communal space in which the entire company of 200 employees could meet once a week. They also needed social areas for eating, working and hanging out, and smaller places to meet and develop ideas and new drink concepts. Since Stiff + Trevillion constructed the building that would house Innocent, the designers knew how to approach the challenge of creating a space big enough for company-wide meetings. They removed part of one of the floor plates, leaving a double-height area flooded with light and surrounded with communal areas.

The resulting spaces look nothing like an office, but more like a park. Picnic tables sit on a carpeting of grass and streamers hang from the balcony. Bright colors abound and reminders of the company's juicy products and their fresh ingredients are everywhere. The new Innocent offices certainly do turn the concept of office design on its head.

Picnic tables, green grass and streamers are an immediate indication that this is no ordinary office.

Product innovation and fun go hand-in-hand at Innocent. A kitchen is located right next to the large communal area.

Innocent needed a space large enough for the entire company to meet. The designers removed part of a floor plate to create this double-height communal area.

A second-story balcony encircles the communal area. Here are located meeting rooms, library, gym, changing rooms and quiet meeting/working areas.

The quirky and fun nature of Innocent is apparent throughout the offices.

DESIGN: **Stiff + Trevillion Architects**, London, UK
CLIENT: **Innocent**
CONTRACTOR: **Parkeray**
LIGHTING: **Atrium**
PHOTOGRAPHY: **Kilian O'Sullivan**

Interceramic

Garland, TX

Michael Malone Architects, Inc., Dallas, TX

Interceramic is one of the largest manufacturers of ceramic tile in North America. Based in Chihuahua, Mexico the company recently decided to build a plant in the United States, contrary to what many feared would be fostered by NAFTA. In addition to manufacturing tile, the company distributes natural stone and tile manufactured by other companies. Interceramic's US presence also includes showrooms and distribution centers.

Michael Malone Architects was contracted to design and build a new 30,000 sq. ft. space that would house the company's 60 office workers. "Interceramic wanted to convey that they were a progressive and sophisticated company with superior products who were making a significant commitment and investment in the United States," states principal Michael Malone. "The plant, to which the offices are attached, is one of the most technologically complex and highly automated in the world. Consideration of this commitment to thought leadership also extended to the kind of environment they wanted to provide to their staff. Even though the offices were built in a manufacturing environment, they are open, light filled and encourage circulation and casual interaction."

Interceramic also wanted to utilize their new offices to

showcase their products. To that end tile is used extensively, not only as flooring, but also for walls and other surfaces. Stone imported by Interceramic is also seen throughout—used for wall and column covers, and counter and tabletops.

"Using tile and stone in new and different ways and making them stand out in the space was a central challenge of the project," says Malone. "To contrast with the density and depth of these materials we used maple for paneling, wood trim and accents and much of the custom furniture. The quiet nature of the maple allowed the tile and stone to be the focus of the design, while providing much needed warmth and visual relief."

Because the space designated for the offices was an appendage to the manufacturing plant—appropriate to its surroundings and the utilitarian nature of the operation—it had few windows and a constrained footprint. The designers confronted these challenges by inserting a sky-lit central atrium space. This space also provides the primary vertical circulation in the form of an open stair. The atrium is adjacent to the entry which doubles as a showroom for Interceramic products. At the upper level of the atrium a large central conference room with glass walls that allow light to flow into the atrium space from the perimeter.

The central atrium is the most striking visual feature of the offices. Within this sky-lit space are located the curving reception desk, and the primary vertical circulation in the form of an architectural stair.

Seating areas for informal breakouts and meetings are arranged around the atrium. Black marble panels are mounted to steel framing and support the skylight above the atrium, which allows natural light to flood the space. Maple is used to contrast with the dark floor tile and marble wall panels.

Custom designed carrels flank a seating area outside the executive suite. Interceramic leadership has offices in this area where maple is again used to contrast with tile and stone products.

The upper level of the atrium provides access to a large conference room that is enclosed in glass to allow natural light to flow through the room and into the atrium. A custom conference table showcases the company's natural stone products.

The reception area doubles as a showroom for Interceramic's tile and natural stone offerings. The reception desk is in the atrium and beneath the skylight at the heart of the building.

Tile is used for flooring even in office areas, above left, allowing the company to showcase the tile's beauty and durability. In the showroom, above right, the neutrality and warmth of maple again contrasts Interceramic's products.

DESIGN: **Michael Malone Architects, Inc.,** Dallas, TX
Michael Malone, AIA, Design Principal
David Droese, AIA, Project Manager
Bob Borson, AIA
Michael Hsu, AIA
Michael Stoddard, AIA
CLIENT: **Interceramic**
CONTRACTOR: **Michael Malone Architects, Inc.**
LIGHTING: **Michael Malone Architects, Inc.**
PHOTOGRAPHY: **Jud Haggard Photography**

Jenterra

Irving, TX

The Michael Malone Studio at WKMC Architects, Dallas, TX

New glass entry portals provide access to the newly created atrium.

JFO is a privately owned holding company with several portfolio businesses beneath its umbrella. JFO shares some services and support structures with three other companies and a large philanthropy—each requiring office space to house their operations. An 80,000 sq. ft. building, Jenterra, was acquired by JFO and remodeled by The Michael Malone Studio at WKMC Architects to accommodate the needs of the combined workforce of approximately 200 employees.

JFO and its portfolio companies are committed to empowering the individual and to helping each staff member achieve their fullest potential within the enterprise. Although the owners wanted each of the diverse companies and their staff member to have a defined home within the new building, they also wanted to create a shared identity and

Bridges span each end of the atrium and provide access to the cantilevered helical stairs. Offices along the perimeter of the atrium receive natural light from the roof monitor.

The dramatic helical stairs encourage people to walk from floor to floor. The offices along the perimeter of the atrium are animated by views of colleagues moving through the space—thereby eliminating the feeling of isolation. The atrium allows each employee access to natural light and a pleasant place to break and enjoy a meal.

The top level of the atrium is open to the roof monitor and a continuous fourth-level promenade. A central bridge spans the atrium at this level.

Bridges at each end of the atrium provide access to the stairs and areas for informal meetings.

opportunities for collaboration and interaction. To achieve the needed connection within separation, the idea of an atrium was developed.

Principal Michael Malone explains, "In conjunction with the owner we realized early on in the design process that to generate the interaction and collaboration between separate entities they desired would be impossible in the context of a typical office floor plate. The idea of a central gathering space in the form of an atrium was floated and embraced, despite the fact it would require removal of potentially leasable floor area. The atrium was literally carved from former office floor plate. Once this decision was made the two sides of the building were knit together horizontally with bridges that cross the ends of the space, and vertically with the dramatic, cantilevered helical stairs."

The atrium is a place of entry and meeting—a space that everyone has to traverse to go to and from their offices and to other parts of the building. Light floods the space from a rooftop monitor that caps the building and provides ample natural lighting to supplement traditional electrical lighting. The striking sculptural staircase encourages vertical circulation—on foot—and chance encounters, promoting a more active, healthier and enjoyable workplace.

DESIGN: **The Michael Malone Studio at WKMC Architects,** Dallas, TX
Michael Malone, AIA, Principal
Paul Pascarelli, AIA, Project Manager
Steven Domingue, AIA, Project Architect
CLIENT: **JFO**
STRUCTURAL ENGINEER: **Stenstrom Schneider, Inc.**
LANDSCAPE ARCHITECT: **MESA Design Group**
CONTRACTOR: **Martin Ringle Construction**
PROJECT MANAGEMENT CONSULTANT: **Steven Jarvis**
LIGHTING: **The Michael Malone Studio at WKMC Architects**
PHOTOGRAPHY: **Jud Haggard Photography**

JPC Architects
Bellevue, WA

JPC Architects, Bellevue, WA

When planning for their new offices, JPC Architects, an architectural and design services firm located in Bellevue, WA, knew what they wanted. As a design firm, it was important for their new space to foster collaboration. They wanted to minimize any barriers that would limit innovation. JPC's former space had an existing floor plan from a prior tenant with tall partitions, limited sight lines, and a floor plan that was a maze.

With their recent relocation all of that changed. The new office is a collaborative environment that enhances group creativity and staff wellbeing. JPC's new award winning space is environmentally friendly and acts as a "design laboratory" for client-centered innovation.

Most of the office and staff are visible at a glance in the new studio space. There are fewer private offices and those that remain are located in the interior and have glass fronts and doors. Desk partitions are low, allowing natural light to flood the entire space and most of the workstations have views of the outside. To maximize collaboration, circulation paths take staff members past each other's desks and there are a number of spaces that facilitate breakout sessions and impromptu conversations.

The shape of the 10,000 sq. ft. space did present a challenge. Designed for several retail tenants, it was exceptionally deep with a long, narrow entryway. The designers met the challenge by transforming the long entryway into a branding experience through which guests travel to reach the reception desk. Along the way is a gallery of the firm's work. The designers also located two large conference rooms and the kitchen in what were the retail storefronts, ensuring a connection to the outdoors and adjacent courtyard.

The designers turned the office's long, narrow entryway, this page and opposite, into a gallery experience.

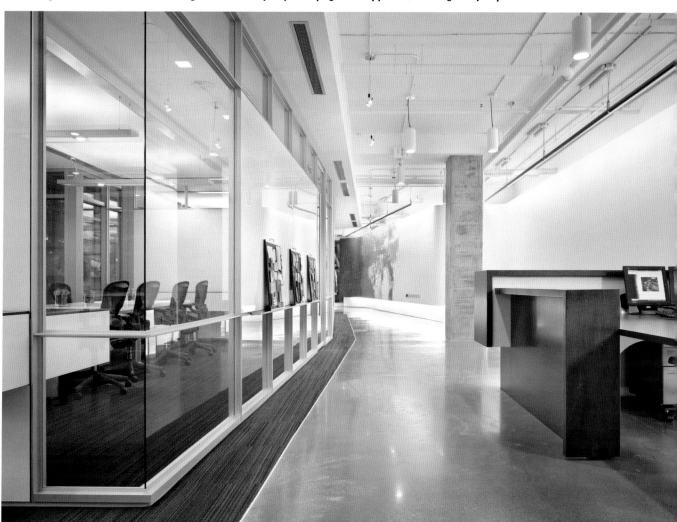

A conference room, above, and kitchen, below, are located in what were formerly retail storefronts—showcasing the firm to passersby and providing employees and guests floor-to-ceiling views of the street.

The gray-scale color palette and open-office plan provide an environment in which the office acts as a backdrop for the more important designs-in-progress. JPC's new office is environmentally friendly and has received a LEED Silver rating.

DESIGN: **JPC Architects**, Bellevue, WA
CLIENT: **JPC Architects**
CONTRACTOR: **Foushee**
PHOTOGRAPHY: **Benjamin Benschneider**

LBi

Brick Lane, East London, UK

Brinkworth, London, UK

The entire rear of the building has been glazed, allowing light to flood the space.

LBi, a global marketing and technology agency headquartered in London, wanted to give what were separate teams in various sites across the city a single place to call their own. They needed an environment that would reflect LBi's position as a leader in the tech-driven world of 21st century branding and provide its 500 employees with ample room to create.

LBi got its start in the early days of digital communications and today prides itself on digital expertise that is second to none. To house its diverse team of experts the agency wanted a large, one-of-a kind space, utterly unlike the usual corporate office. If clients were to trust the company to lead them into the future, then LBi needed to look the part of a cool, smart, young, and ultra creative company.

To do this the company, ironically, borrowed cachet from the past and converted an historic building—the Atlantis Building, part of the Truman Brewery site in London—into their new workplace. Constructed as the brewing halls for the Hanbury Truman brewing family, the 60,000 sq. ft. space has more recently been used for events and exhibitions and had become an integral part of the increasingly hip quarter of Spitalfields and Brick Lane.

The design, by London firm Brinkworth, began with the original industrial shell and transformed it into a spacious, contemporary and light-filled office. Portions of the original façade were left in place while other sections were replaced with full-height glazing. The entire rear of the building was glazed to flood the space with light and allow views over East London.

The heart of the building is a three-story atrium that houses reception and greets quests with a dramatic mixture

The dramatic reception atrium with a cut-out that makes the basement level an integral part of the new space.

The three-story atrium as seen from the ground level and from the basement. The large, flexible basement includes an auditorium for presentations, a café, game rooms, white-tiled shower spaces and bathrooms—all things to give creative types some time to mingle and relax.

of the historic structure and contemporary design. To create this huge space the designers cut back the floor slab opening the basement level to the main floor. Drama alone, however, cannot fulfill the needs of LBi's many clients, and studio space and flexible meeting areas had to be created. To do so, the structure of the building was altered to add mezzanine levels—and extend existing ones—within the almost 33 ft. high (ten meter) space.

"The bridge over the basement void and the suspended bridge that connects the first floor and the new first floor mezzanine level, contribute to making this a dynamic entrance to LBi's office space," states Brinkworth's Associate Director Murray Aitken. "This alteration of the building's fabric enhances the volume of the space, particularly the generous height and expresses the new levels as separate entities within the existing structure, while maximizing the available workspace," he continues.

Instead of introducing structural columns to support the new mezzanine floors and compromising the usable space underneath, the designers chose to hang the floors from the massive existing structural frame. This solution allowed for open-plan workplaces on both levels and maximum flexibility.

Throughout the new space the designers' simple yet dynamic approach has ensured that the integrity of the former brewing halls has been retained throughout while creating space for 500 people and creating an environment that reflects LBi's brand.

Contemporary meeting areas and studio spaces are set within the original structure, incorporating old and new elements while in the process giving the company's 500 employees room to exchange ideas and create.

Elements from the original industrial building, including pipe work, are retained throughout. Complementing the industrial look are raw metal finishes and strong accent colors.

DESIGN: **Brinkworth**, London, UK
CLIENT: **LBi**
PHOTOGRAPHY: **Alex Franklin**

Leo Burnett Office

Singapore

Ministry of Design, Singapore

Singapore's Ministry of Design was recently entrusted with the design of a new Singapore office for famed advertising agency Leo Burnett, one of the largest advertising networks in the world. The new, second-floor space needed to nurture the creativity and innovation for which the agency is known and maintain the people-centric approach on which it has always focused.

The designers divided their task, and the office, into three sections: Space to Impress, Space to Interact, and Space to Create. The Space to Impress encompasses the reception area and entrance foyer and it certainly does impress. Greeting employees and visitors as they step out of the elevator is a huge, wall-filling drawing of the iconic ad man himself, Leo Burnett. The graffiti-style portrait, almost ten

The stately exterior. Leo Burnett is on the second floor.

The energetic line work captures the man behind the famous agency and, simultaneously, the creativity and energy with which the agency is associated.

A chill-out space includes a wheelbarrow full of trophies. A reminder of the agency's many successes.

feet high (three meters), is not contained to the walls, but splashes over the windows, ceiling and floor. A vastly-oversized pencil, running floor to ceiling and placed as if it has just completed the portrait, represents the active nature of drawing and creativity itself.

The next area, the Space to Interact, includes informal areas for employees and clients to hang out and relax as well as more formal meeting rooms. Together the formal and informal offer a variety of possibilities for groups, large and small, to gather and exchange ideas. Also included in this area is a projection wall on which ideas can be illustrated on a grand scale. While the formal meeting rooms are private, peek-o-boo portholes on the walls allow glimpses of the work going on inside—dispelling the idea of creativity taking place behind closed doors.

The last area, the Space to Create, is the actual work area. In this large open space the creative talent is united around a series of open-plan desks that allow for individuals to either collaborate or concentrate on their own. Custom-designed plywood tabletops of various colors form a playful checkerboard pattern that lightens the mood and increases the energy level of the space. As an alternative, staff can work, or take a break, on an outdoor deck that is just steps away.

Apples, an integral part of Leo Burnett's history, are offered from bowls and included in a feature wall. (The story goes that when Leo Burnett opened his agency during the depths of the Great Depression in 1935, a newspaper critic predicted that the new agency would fail and that Burnett would be reduced to selling apples on the street. Having proved the naysayer wrong Burnett and his agency have offered apples to visitors and employees ever since.)

Employee capacity at Leo Burnett Singapore's new office is 112 persons and the total floor area is 13,778 sq. ft. (1,280 sq. meters).

The Space to Interact includes informal areas with more formal meeting rooms. These rooms have green, back-painted glass and portholes that allow glimpses of the work going on inside. Technology includes a projection wall and counter-mounted monitors.

Furniture is located to allow people to meet in groups large and small. A feature wall includes the apples that are of historic importance to the agency. The Space to Create, below right, is an open-plan work area with custom-designed plywood tables.

INTERIOR ARCHITECTURE AND DESIGN: **Ministry of Design**, Singapore
HEAD DESIGNER: **Colin Seah**
DESIGNERS: **Kevin Leong, Roberto Rivera, Lolleth Alejandro, Sacharissa Kurniawan, Don Castaneda**
STRUCTURAL CONSULTANT: **CME Engineering Pte Ltd**
CONTRACTOR: **Kingsdec Interior**
CLIENT: **Leo Burnett, Singapore**
PHOTOGRAPHY: **CI&A Photography, Edward Hendricks**

Losan Group
Coruña, Spain

Marcos Samaniego / MAS · ARQUITECTURA
Coruña, Spain

Losan Group, a leading Spanish manufacturer of wood products, recently selected MAS • ARQUITECTURA, also of Spain, to renovate Losan's main office and create more usable work area within the limited space. Important to the client was that the spirit of the multinational company be communicated through the design of the office.

Losan's beautiful products are, of course, utilized everywhere one looks. The dramatic reception area is entirely lined in wood—walls, floor and ceiling—and even the upholstered chairs are encircled with wood strips. Adding movement to the space, and preventing any hint of monotony, is the diversity of application. Floor planks vary in direction from one end of room to the other and contrast with the vertical strips in the furniture. Irregularly-spaced

cut-outs on the wall—and on other walls throughout the office—create a contemporary, decorative pattern.

The attention to detail found in the reception area is carried throughout the rest of the office, including the corridor, meeting rooms and work spaces. Even the restrooms and a small coffee room get careful attention from the designers. Natural light is an important element in the design. Windows are carefully placed to capture light and take advantage of the pleasant views, adding to the employee satisfaction and quality of life.

The resulting office artfully displays Losan Group's high-quality products and provides an interesting and stimulating work environment.

The entry area is lined with solid wood. A shelving unit to one side showcases the company's products—each on its own individually-lit shelf.

124

The stunning reception area glows with warmth and natural light.

In the board room, above and below left, a solid wood table sits under beams of the same material. Meeting rooms and offices throughout the space incorporate wood and light to improve the working environment for both visitors and employees.

Far from being overlooked, the restrooms are a thing of beauty and include more warm wood, soft colors and, above the doors, identifying portraits of a king and queen. Corridors, offices and even a small coffee room are also lined with wood.

DESIGN: **Marcos Samaniego / MAS • ARQUITECTURA**, Coruña, Spain
PHOTOGRAPHY: **Ana Samaniego**

M Financial Group
Portland, OR

Yost Grube Hall Architecture
Portland, OR

M Financial Group is a successful, nationwide organization which serves the needs of affluent individuals and highly successful companies. M wanted to increase their market presence and create a space that reflected their progressive clientele. Because of its persistent growth, the company recently relocated its headquarters to Portland's vibrant Pearl District.

Yost Grube Hall Architecture was tasked with the design of M Financial's new, 56,000 sq. ft. space located within the top three-floors of a ten-story building.

True to M Financial's Northwestern heritage, the completed design features the beauty and simplicity of natural materials including large expanses of stone, bamboo, maple and curupixa. "The restrained pallette of quality finishes was paramount to convey the company's preferred image," said Scott Brown, director of interior design at Yost Grube Hall Architecture. "It's a balance of color and subtle textures which yielded a professional, yet corporate environment."

Linking the three floors is a dramatic internal staircase. The stair encircles a 40-foot water feature which poetically

The main lobby offers spectacular views of the skyline and an axial connection to one of Portland's most iconic bridges.

An internal stair connects the three
floors and encircles a water feature.

Important to M Financial was the inclusion of many areas for employees to interact away from the intense concentration of their workspaces. A break out space, above, offers just such an opportunity. Comfortable seating, views of the city and the play of natural light promote interchange. The understated elegance of natural wood is found here as well as in private offices and conference rooms, below.

A coffee bar is one of the amenities offered within the 8,000 sq. ft. of public interaction space.

reinforced the company's Northwestern location and introduced rhythmic motion and sound. In addition to windows offering stunning views and natural light at almost every turn, there are 12 skylights allowing in additional light. A play of various contrasts—horizontal and vertical planes; opacity and transparency—add interest without adding complications to the design.

Important to the client was the inclusion of spaces for employees to gather, away from the concentrated efforts of their own desks—a recognition that staff need a variety of spaces to thrive. A coffee bar is one of the amenities provided for this interaction. The lunchroom, an outdoor terrace, and the water feature also provide the essential gathering spots to support interaction.

ARCHITECT: **Yost Grube Hall Architecture,** Portland, OR
CLIENT: **M Financial Group**
CONTRACTOR: **Hoffman Construction**
STRUCTURAL ENGINEER: **KPFF Consulting Engineers**
MECHANICAL/ELECTRICAL ENGINEER: **Glumac**
LIGHTING: **Pacific Lightworks**
PHOTOGRAPHY: **Pete Eckert, Eckert & Eckert Photography**

Mason Capital Management
New York, NY

Spector Group, New York, NY; Woodbury, NY

Employees of Mason Capital Management, a hedge fund established in 2000, have happily discovered that their new, two-floor, 25,000 sq. ft. midtown Manhattan office keeps youthful, talented and high-powered individuals working effectively, sharing information, and feeling inspired. The award-winning contemporary space, which includes a reception area, private offices, open workstations, trading desks, boardroom, conference rooms, data center, fitness center, showers and lockers, has been designed by Spector Group as a distinctive blend of form and function.

As a workplace, the facility maximizes productivity with an efficient floor plan, unimpeded visibility (through low-height workstations, glass-enclosed private offices and conference rooms, and trading desks aligned for eye-to-eye contact among traders), energy saving LED lighting fixtures, and green building materials such as wood, metal, stone, glass and leather. Yet the design is also an attractive, progressive and thought-provoking environment, playing finely milled and elegantly finished wood paneling against raw steel and concrete floors, raising and lowering the ceiling plane through coves and soffits, intermingling ergonomic furniture with striking avant-garde pieces, and presenting the interconnecting stair as a cutting edge sculptural composition of translucent resin treads and glass railings to stimulate use by employees. Coming to work should always be this rewarding.

An interconnecting stair near the reception area serves as a cutting edge sculptural element.

The facility includes glass-enclosed conference rooms, above, and trading desks aligned for eye-to-eye contact among traders, below.

DESIGN: **Spector Group**, New York, NY; Woodbury, NY
CLIENT: **Mason Capital Management,** New York, NY
PHOTOGRAPHY: **Eric Laignel**
TEXT: **Roger Yee**

MNProgram
Coruña, Spain

Marcos Samaniego / MAS · ARQUITECTURA, Coruña, Spain

One would never guess from the entrance to the office that the other side of the building looks over the Atlantic Ocean. Contrasting elements in the office include natural wood and contemporary furnishings. Below is the reception desk.

"The Ring" provides employees with a place to meet and work that is mentally and spatially removed from their everyday desks, providing a fresh outlook and a warming, natural ambience.

MNProgram, a leading management software company located in Spain recently hired MAS • ARQUITECTURA to design the new MNProgram office. The design combines functionality with highly unusual elements inspired by the natural world. The resulting space enables employees to both work and relax—therefore optimizing productivity.

Perhaps the most obvious manifestation of the natural world is the stunning view over the Atlantic Ocean from a bank of windows. Although not, strictly speaking, the work of designer Marcos Samaniego, he did allow this valuable natural setting to influence his vision for the space.

The center piece of the design is "the ring." Set amidst the white, modern tables, desks and chairs of the workstations, this raised, square enclosure—made of wood—dominates the central area of the office. It offers a relaxing space for creative thought and interchange, away from the normal routine of the workstations.

Also built from wood are a whimsical "bridge" that leads to the restrooms and a small room—entirely lined in wood from floor to ceiling—that's meant only for relaxation. In it are a sofa, a TV and a kitchen area. The designer didn't stop there in his pursuit of the natural world. Underpinning "the ring" and covering several floor spaces and even a wall, is soft, green grass. The combination of grass and natural-colored wood is hard to resist.

In the open-plan work area, workstations are positioned longitudinally to take best advantage of the natural light and provide easy movement and direct site lines. Taken together, the nearby ocean, the high-quality, satin-finish furnishings and the natural elements, the new MNProgram office is by all accounts a great place to spend the workday.

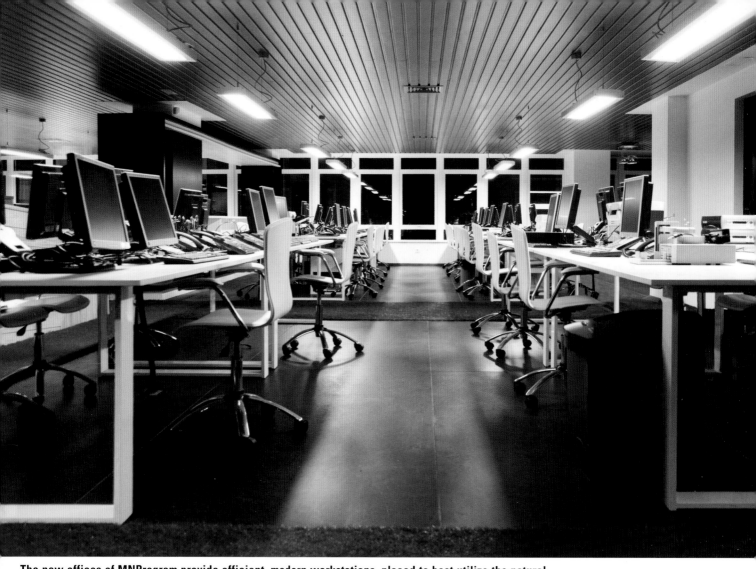

The new offices of MNProgram provide efficient, modern workstations, placed to best utilize the natural light. Not visible here, but right outside the windows, is the Atlantic Ocean.

The designers built several elements within the space from natural wood. A foot bridge leads to the restrooms and a small room, lined entirely in wood, holds a sofa, TV and kitchen area. Lining the floors and one wall—and complementing the natural wood—is a field of grass.

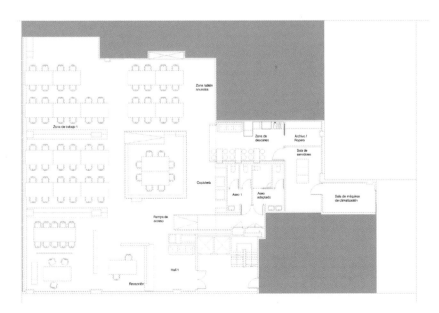

DESIGN: **Marcos Samaniego / MAS • ARQUITECTURA**, Coruña, Spain
CLIENT: **MNProgram**
PHOTOGRAPHY: **Ana Samaniego**

National Parks Conservation Association

Washington, DC

OTJ Architects, Washington, DC

The National Parks Conservation Association (NPCA) is a nonprofit organization that works to ensure that America's national parks receive the care and support they need. The association believes emphatically that national parks and historical sites are vital to the plant and animal species that inhabit them as well as the human visitors that find inspiration and peace within their boundaries.

This concern for the natural environment extended to the association's approach to the recent relocation of its Washington, DC offices. The driving force behind every aspect of the planning, design, construction, and continued use of the new space was the protection of the environment, health, and welfare of the association's employees and guests.

From the very beginning of the process, NPCA worked closely with the designers at OTJ Architects, as well as the real estate, engineering and construction companies involved, to secure LEED-CI certification and ensure the new office had as little negative impact on the environment as possible. Lida Lewis of OTJ states, "Multiple staff members had previously had exposure to green buildings, and the nature of their mission as an organization made LEED and

green building design a clear area for intensive investigation. Because of this early focus, building site selection was a major component of the process."

NPCA, along with real estate company, West, Lane, & Schlager Realty Advisors, targeted buildings in dense, urban areas of downtown DC with easy access to multiple modes of transportation and strong sustainable services already in place. The final selection was a space on the sixth and seventh floors of an 11-story building in the Chinatown neighborhood. The location has an abundance of natural light, a multi-level garage below grade, access to multiple public transportation options, and a large selection of nearby restaurants.

The long, narrow floor plan and wide adjacent streets results in natural light exposure on all of the building's facades. The design was carefully planned to take full advantage of the natural light, saving energy and enriching the workplace environment. To keep the perimeter open and available to staff, spaces which require solid walls are grouped around the building's existing compact core service block. Areas which require some, but not primary, access to

Green building practices reign supreme. In the reception area high post-consumer recycled content wood-textured ceramic tile, sustainably produced wood flooring, reclaimed barn wood wall surfaces and locally quarried stone veneer produce a warm and inviting space.

NPCA wants to encourage an easy access, "open-door" policy for all employees. Even the workstations of senior management, such as the president, above, have low-height panels. An internal staircase, below left, leads from the reception area to the library/meeting area. A system of Plexiglas panels, below right, is reminiscent of the natural beauty that the association works so hard to preserve.

light, such as the main conference space and the lunchroom, are arranged along the side of the building that faces a somewhat narrow alley. This leaves the spaces with the most direct sunlight open for staff areas.

An open office plan, with low workstation panels, ensures that even staff not directly adjacent to the windows get an abundance of light. Team rooms are located in the corners and directly along the windows to allow employees to meet in the most sun-filled areas. These rooms are enclosed with clear-vision glass. Additional lighting is provided with carefully selected fluorescent lighting and LED lighting fixtures. In the open workspaces, the designers sourced a brand of fixture—Ledalite—in which 95% of the light generated by the fixture passes through the lens and into the space.

To support the open-office plan, there are many spaces for collaboration. Conference rooms of varying sizes, several small team rooms, and a centralized lunchroom with a variety of seating types all foster formal and informal teamwork.

Acoustical comfort was also determined to be critical to the success of the open environment. Minimizing the sound level are workstation panels with sound-absorptive cores, carpeted flooring and sound absorptive ceiling tiles. Areas prone to excessive noise generation are enclosed with thick, sound-controlling partitions and a soundmasking system is utilized in the open workstation areas.

To further enhance the experience and health of employees, much attention was given to green construction and

"While NPCA's former facility had been an open office environment, very tall workstation panels and unclear spatial organization had, over time, established a very isolative environment," explains Lewis. "There was much initial apprehension and concern over adopting a more open, seated-height partition environment, despite the desire for all staff members to be able to have access to the abundance of natural light afforded by the narrow floorplate. Three dimensional modeling and visits to area furniture showrooms helped to alleviate these fears. Ultimately, the incorporation of glazed panels into the workstations and the lowering of the panel heights have been considered a clear success. The new facility's clear, open site lines and access to views and light on every façade have already begun, according to the staff, to forge new and stronger connections between staff members and departments."

An early design directive was to make an office space which would make staff and visitors feel as if they had "walked right into" NPCA's award-winning magazine, *National Parks*. To that end displays of park artwork are found in the pantry above, and throughout the space. Bright punches of green, yellow and chocolate brown enliven the space and are pulled from the organization's branding guidelines.

housekeeping practices, both during construction and for continued maintenance. Low emitting materials were given priority to ensure the healthiest possible working environment and air quality testing was carried out by a third party prior to occupancy.

All materials were evaluated to maximize pre- and post-consumer content, localized manufacturing, and low emissions. Modular carpeting manufactured by Interface allows the replacement of single tiles if damaged, eliminating the need to replace an entire area of carpeting. Also attractive to NPCA was Interface's dedication to reducing, and by 2020 eliminating, any negative impact the company has on the environment.

All this attention to protecting the environment did not stop at completion of the project. NPCA has in place a strict sustainable purchasing policy for food products at all catered events in the office, annual meetings, annual off-site meetings, and foodstuffs provided in the lunchroom. To reduce the environmental and transportation impacts associated with food production and distribution, NPCA is committed to achieving a sustainable purchase threshold of at least 25% of total combined food and beverage purchases (by cost)

annually. Items must be either sustainably labeled or harvested or produced within a 100-mile radius of the NPCA office. Each source company must also have a commitment to larger environmental goals and to the greater public good.

"The careful collaboration of NPCA, OTJ Architects, GPI, Engineering, *rand Construction, West, Lane & Schlager Realty Advisors, and CBRE was of vital importance to the strong focus of all parties towards the goal of constructing a fresh new green facility for the National Parks Conservation Association's headquarters in Chinatown," concludes Lewis. "The project team anticipates that this new office space will serve to enhance the experience of all NPCA employees and guests, by providing greater access to natural light, low exposure to toxic materials, a lowered carbon footprint for the office's construction and operations, low energy consumption, and access to a vibrant, dense community with a plethora of alternative commuting opportunities."

DESIGN: **OTJ Architects,** Washington, DC
CLIENT: **National Parks Conservation Association**
CONTRACTOR: ***rand Construction**
ENGINEER: **Greenman-Pedersen, Inc. & Old Town Engineering**
COMMISSIONING & IAQ CONSULTANT: **Healthy Buildings**
PHOTOGRAPHY: **Chris Spielmann, Spielmann Studio**

Obscura Digital

San Francisco, CA

IwamotoScott Architecture, San Francisco, CA

Obscura Digital is a cutting-edge immersive and interactive media company that creates three dimensional projections, and builds mapping, art, graphics and multi-touch interfaces. It operates both at the forefront of technology and with a scrappy, can-do attitude—its employees make things work through inventive and original thinking. When Obscura tasked IwamotoScott Architecture with the design of its San Francisco office, it was vital that the space fully support the creative nature of the business and the staff.

The results are truly commanding. The soaring ceilings and visible structural skeleton are practical for a company with extensive technical needs and metaphorically fitting for their continual advancement into the tech-driven world of communications. On the practical side, Obscura wanted to connect a large prototyping area on the lower level to their main production facilities located above. They also needed an impressive place to bring clients that would truly show-

case their work and define them as a company to be trusted with the most advanced projects.

To create the needed communication between levels, the designers cut a hole in the floor and added an internal staircase. An impressive conference room was embedded in the structural steel of the building. It acts as a showpiece in and of itself while affording clients and guests views over the prototyping and showroom area. General work areas are large and open, providing employees access to natural light and each other.

The designers chose inexpensive raw and off-the-shelf materials, but used them in innovative ways, assuring that visitors see only the industrial-chic ambiance. Combining utility and style, a custom designed storage unit doubles as a projection wall and fills one end of the long, open two-story space. The new space is as impressive as the company's creative output.

The impressive entry leads to the upper level of the two-level space.

The new conference room sits slightly elevated from its surroundings. The lower-level showroom, below, offers various diversions.

The designers used inexpensive materials in creative ways, such as the "twisting" office walls and the re-purposed stair railing.

The geodesic dome seen in the foreground is used for 360 degree projections. The conference room sits beyond the new stair. An innovative wall, below, that acts as both a projection wall and storage unit, occupies one end of the space.

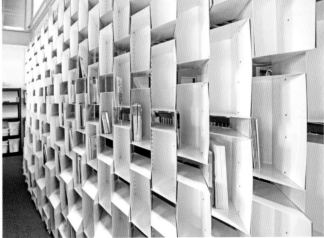

The conference room is encased in the building's structural framework. The room affords guests and clients a view of the prototyping area and serves to brand Obscura Digital as a cutting-edge company of innovative thinkers.

An open-space office has wood, steel and concrete much in evidence. Many of the surfaces, below, bend and weave.

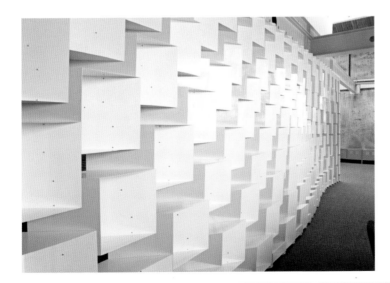

DESIGN: **IwamotoScott Architecture**, San Francisco, CA
CLIENT: **Obscura Digital,** San Francisco, CA
PHOTOGRAPHY: **Rien van Rijthoven**

Office Herengracht

Amsterdam, The Netherlands

i29 interior architects, Amsterdam, The Netherlands
Eckhardt & Leeuwenstein Architects, Amsterdam, The Netherlands

The board of an investment group in Amsterdam (client's name withheld) wanted what they called a "power office." The group tasked two firms—i29 interior architects and Eckhardt & Leeuwenstein Architects, both of Amsterdam—to create the needed office in an historic, 17th Century building along *de gouden bocht,* or golden bend, one of Amsterdam's most famous canals. The designers used gold as their inspiration and collaborated to create a playful design that put each board member in the spotlight—literally.

In three boardrooms, the spotlights in question are cast from large, round lampshades—painted gold on the inside—that hang from the ceiling. Each lamp appears to cast a large spotlight across the room. This effect is created with artfully painted walls and furniture and large ovals of differing shades of gray carpet. Golden ovals on the black-stained walls are actually cabinets and shelving set in oval cut-outs. The basic color palette of black and white heightens the effect of the golden spotlights.

Although the three boardrooms and the lounge are executed with the same overall design concept, only the boardrooms get the golden treatment. In the lounge, silver—inside the lampshades and patterned over the furniture—replaces the gold and a white marble floor adds richness. The lounge can also be used for presentations and events and includes an integrated flat screen in the bar and data connections in each piece of furniture.

Throughout the office, gold and silver and their creative application playfully serve a company concerned with money and power.

The lounge area is executed in white, black and silver. Elegant details from the 17th century building are painted white. A doorway, right, is enclosed in an oval of gold.

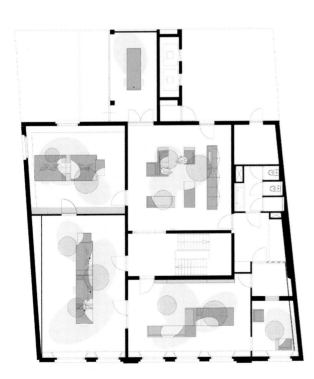

In the boardrooms, spotlights spill over the walls, floor and furniture. The spotlight effect is created with gold paint and patterns of gray carpet. Even the furniture is painted to suggest an oval of light.

DESIGN: **i29 interior architects; Eckhardt & Leeuwenstein Architects,** Amsterdam, The Netherlands
CONTRACTOR: **Van Zoelen bv**
CABINET MAKER: **Jehago bv**
CLIENT: **Office Herengracht,** Amsterdam, The Netherlands
PHOTOGRAPHY: **i29 interior architects**

Palazzo Advisory & Acquisitions

New York, NY

CCS Architecture, New York, NY

Palazzo Advisory & Acquisitions is a boutique acquisitions and investment bank that is singularly focused on creating value and wealth for its clients who, according to the company's literature, are "owners and stakeholders of marketing services, interactive, digital, information, and new media companies." When tasking CCS Architecture with the design of its 3,000 sq. ft. office in midtown Manhattan, paramount importance was given to the creation of a space that was sophisticated and modern without feeling cold and corporate. Clients had to feel at ease, but completely confident in the soundness of Palazzo's advice.

The first area greeting visitors, the reception area, encapsulates the design of the office and immediately communicates the tenor of the company. It is spacious with rich finishes that evoke a sense of luxury and a slight reference to boardrooms of financial institutions. Visible in its entirety from the reception area is a conference room fronted in glass and backed with a wall of rich wood—made richer with subtle lighting patterns. A sleek table and chairs and the lack of any distracting decoration gives the room a modern appeal and underpins the expertise and skill of the firm's services.

The reception area greets visitors with a sea of rich wood. The wood floor flows onto the back wall of a nearby, clear-glass enclosed conference room.

The sumptuous conference room.

The office includes views of the upscale 57th Street location, subtly highlighting the firm's expertise at wealth creation. Glass partitions afford privacy for the staff of ten, while conveying the idea of transparency. Contemporary furnishes add comfort and understated elegance.

DESIGN: **CCS Architecture,** New York, NY
DESIGN PRINCIPAL: **Cass Calder Smith**
PROJECT ARCHITECT: **Stephanie Kinnick**
CONTRACTOR: **OMEGA Construction + Design**
CLIENT: **Palazzo Advisory & Acquisitions,** New York, NY
PHOTOGRAPHY: **Paul Dyer**

plajer & franz studio

Berlin, Germany

plajer & franz studio, Berlin, Germany

Much that defines the design of the studio is found in the reception area: elements from the original building, a largely monochromatic color scheme, and concealed storage units. The curved wall is covered in Alcantara.

The heart of the studio is the open kitchen found on the lower level. This is where the architects and designers come together to exchange ideas in a relaxed and social atmosphere.

plajer & franz studio is a Berlin-based design firm known for their love of detail and sense of style. The home and creative base for the studio's 45 architects and interior and graphic designers is a two-level, 10,700 sq. ft. (1,000 sq. meter) space located in a former industrial complex dating back to 1898. For their own studio the designers, showing a deep respect for the building's original character, developed a contemporary design with a striking mixture of old and new.

This mixture is introduced in the light-flooded reception area—as are many other aspects of the design. It's here that the original, rubbed slab ceiling is first seen, as are the whitewashed stone walls and rough mastic asphalt flooring. Also introduced on the contoured counter and curved wall is the monochromatic color scheme that is used throughout the studio.

The studio doesn't, however, give the impression of being monochromatic. White and light-colored surfaces and dark wood create a neutral background for frequent punches of color provided by individual items of furniture, the studio's many publications and books, and even a colorful fish tank.

The reception area contains, or hides, yet another aspect of the design seen in the entire studio: concealed storage units. As a busy, fully-functional studio, storage space and media equipment are a necessity, but to maintain a clean aesthetic the designers have concealed these vital items in sleek and beautifully designed cabinets and drawers. The

items are at everyone's fingertips, but artfully hidden when not in use.

Communication is key to the success of a modern studio and many features within the plajer & franz's space are designed to enhance the employees' and clients' ability to talk to and understand each other. A large kitchen area on the lower level is just for that purpose, a space where everyone can gather in a relaxed and informal environment to exchange ideas and share meals.

Conference rooms are fronted with frameless glass walls with specially designed door frames that seem to float in mid-air. These dividers provide privacy without the secrecy-suggesting coldness of a solid, closed wall. In many areas of the studio, curtains allow for more, or less, privacy as needed.

Alexander Plajer of plajer & franz says, "We believe that the combination of function and aesthetics as well as the contrast between the industrial character of the building and the sophisticated new interior design, carries our design signature: it's always the rough with the smooth and the hot with the cold, but never the lukewarm."

Another view of the kitchen area with its large, communal table. On special occasions, integrated speakers and media technology can transform the space into a club or home cinema. Floor-to-ceiling sliding doors, that when not in use disappear into the walls, can be used to block access to the rest of the studio.

The two levels of the studio are connected by minimalist, filigree stairs reminiscent of a gangway. Instead of being protected by a conventional railing, the floor opening on the upper level is bordered with high boards and a stylized zen garden. Dynamically positioned vertical light strips connect wall, floor and ceiling, creating an eye-catching element at the end of the stairs and spots of color.

Sleek conference rooms provide privacy without isolation. Media equipment and storage space is concealed in specially designed cabinets and drawers,

A curtain on a semi-circular rail allows the creation of an unusual, round, conference room. The semi-transparent fabric and carpet provide pleasant, subdued acoustics.

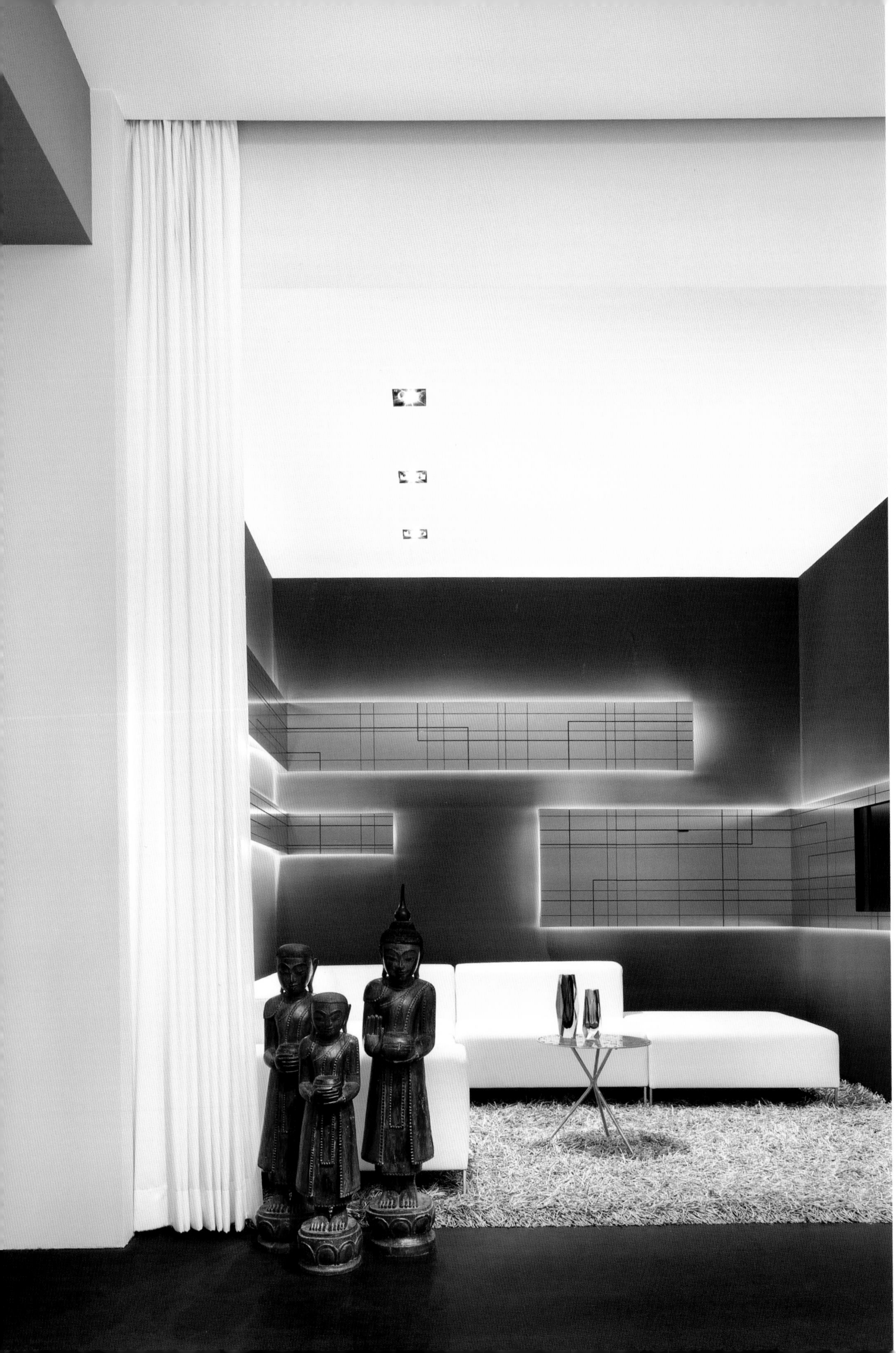

For smaller client meetings, the lounge in the executive office offers a peaceful oasis. The couch, carpet, warm colors and decorative elements create a homey environment. The iridescent blue of a built-in freshwater aquarium adds a soothing effect. Here again, all technology is concealed behind the brass wall panels. The panels surrounding the aquarium can be opened completely for maintenance.

DESIGN: **plajer & franz studio,** Berlin, Germany
CLIENT: **plajer & franz studio,** Berlin, Germany
PHOTOGRAPHY: **Ken Schluchtmann, diephotodesigner.de,** Berlin, Germany

Rossignol

Saint Jean de Moirans, France

Hérault Arnod Architectes, Paris, France

The design captures inspiration from board sports, fluidity of motion as well as natural elements such as snow and glaciers. The building melds perfectly with the mountainous surroundings.

Two materials are used for the external envelope, wood and glass. The structure is made of steel, like an organic skeleton that outlines the shape.

Rossignol is an historic leader in the world of skiing and is intimately linked to the mountains and snow. Their new global headquarters is far from the typical office building. It pays tribute to nature and to technology, which is inseparable from top-level sport. Situated on former farmland, flat and marshy, the firm's headquarters is surrounded by mountains. Creating a fusion of the company's functional and fantasy aspects, the architecture has been specifically designed for Rossignol in a surprising and minimalist form. The design captures inspiration from board sports, fluidity of motion as well as natural elements such as snow and glaciers. To meld perfectly with the mountainous surroundings, the roof envelops the entire project with a tapestry of topography embracing nature and landscape with organic timber-clad shapes.

Previously spread over several locations, Rossignol Group will be assembling different entities in one building to reinforce the "House of Rossignol" brand. Three distinct spaces are located beneath one roof: The racing ski production workshop, the brand's technological showcase, and technical rooms, all grouped alongside the motorway; the office floors which include the administrative and sales departments, R&D, research and design, etc.; and the street, the space of social encounters which crosses the building from one side to the other. At one end, the street widens to become the showroom, spectacular and bright.

The facade creates a kinetic and dynamic effect. The front of the building rises to form a roof over the workshops and then on to the apex, then descends to cover the office area. The irregular profile of the roof and office facades leaves the opportunity for future extensions as required. Additions can be built without disrupting the balance and identity of the project. From the start, the architecture embodies its own growth process.

Inside, the building functions like a "hive" in which the different functions come into contact and interact, where people enjoy the experience of working together and meeting each other. To encourage this internal communication, social spaces are distributed around the building. The restaurant, situated right at the top, is designed as the primary locus for the company life. The building is designed for minimal environmental impact. The technical choices make it an efficient and energy-saving building, well insulated and protected from the summer sun by the timber over-roof. The systems are optimized—the heat produced by the workshop machines is recovered and re-injected into the heating network. The offices receive natural ventilation through automatic window opening.

The roof envelops the entire project with a topography that embraces nature and creates a landscape of organic timber-clad shapes.

The building functions like a "hive" in which the different functions come into contact and interact, where people enjoy the experience of working together and meeting each other.

The facility houses the racing ski production workshop, the brand's technological showcase, and technical rooms.

The restaurant, situated right at the top, is designed as the primary locus for the company life.

DESIGN: **Hérault Arnod Architectes**, Paris, France
PROJECT TEAM: **Jérôme Moenne-Loccoz (project manager), Alexandre Pachiaudi,
Camille Bérar, Nicolas Broussous, Matthias Jäger**
COMPETITION TEAM: **Florent Bellet, Adela Ciurea, Israel Lopez Vargas,
Alexandre Pachiaudi
with François Deslaugiers (for the panoramic lift)**
CLIENT: **Skis Rossignol SAS**
PHOTOGRAPHY: **André Morin, Christian Rausch, Gilles Cabella, Hérault Arnod**

Samsonite Corporation

Mansfield, MA

BKA Architects, Inc., Brockton, MA

Samsonite is a market leader in the design and sale of luggage and travel accessories. Recently the company tasked BKA Architects with the renovation of two floors in an existing building—transforming it into a representative headquarters in which the company's brand identity could be reinforced and where the staff would be proud to work.

Needed was a fresh, global image that would utilize the existing Samsonite corporate identity and maintain the brand's reputation for high-end luxury. The designers were also directed to incorporate a product showroom in the lobby—creating a stunning space that would showcase both the company and its products.

As the existing building lacked the excitement that the client required, a new, two-story lobby was carved out of the structure. The resulting grand and contemporary space features a gray and cream reception desk that displays the corporate logo, a black granite and glass staircase, and product display areas. Dark cherry wood panels add warmth, and the logo is created with inlaid tile in the center of the floor.

In addition to the lobby, BKA designed staff work areas and workstations, management offices, several meeting rooms, a large, multi-purpose room, and a break room—all on the first floor. On the second floor, the work focused on developing representative upper management offices as well as additional conference room space and staff work areas. The second floor meeting room shares a wall of windows with the front of the building and is visible to those entering the building.

According to David Seibert, AIA and Mindy Kaplan of BKA, the greatest challenge and most outstanding aspect of the project regarded the tight schedule and budget. "The greatest innovation was keeping a tight grip on costs and prioritizing the programmatic requirements in order to maximize the budgetary constraints. Unless completely unworkable, the existing architectural components remained, and engineering work was performed on a design/build basis. To aid the client in visualizing the design, BKA developed a conceptual rendering of the space."

The designers' efforts resulted in a headquarters that elevates the brand and its employees.

Both the two-story lobby and a second-level conference room can be seen through the new aluminum and glass façade. The new lobby was carved out of the existing building.

The new two-story entry lobby showcases the Samsonite logo and products. It was a major priority for the client to create a grand space within the existing one-level entrance. The new space reflects the new global corporate philosophy while adhering to a strict construction budget.

A clerestory light well, above, existed in the original structure, however, the designers put its grand scale to better use in the new space. It's now a design element that adds interest and light, rather than just part of a simple corridor, as it was previously. The second floor lobby, below, is located near the two-story entry. Most of the partitions in this space are original to the existing building, with new finishes and lighting.

The new second floor conference room, above, shares a wall of windows with the new entry vestibule. A dropped soffit gives drama and light to the 18-seat conference table. Corporate identity is reinforced in an area outside the main conference room, right.

DESIGN: **BKA Architects, Inc.** Brockton, MA
CLIENT: **Samsonite Corporation**
PROPERTY MANAGER: **Reit Management & Research LLC,** Newton, MA
CONTRACTOR: **Noble Ventures, Inc.** Raynham, MA
FLOORING CONTRACTOR: **Middlesex Carpet Co., Inc.,** Tewksbury, MA
PHOTOGRAPHY: **BKA Architects, Inc.**

schlaich bergermann und partner

Stuttgart, Germany

Ippolito Fleitz Group, Stuttgart, Germany

schlaich bergermann und partner is an engineering firm with an international reputation for building impressive structures such as stadiums and bridges. Headquartered in Stuttgart, the firm has offices in Berlin, New York and Sao Paulo. The Stuttgart team, however, had been spread between two locations and uniting them under one roof was the reason for a recent relocation. Ippolito Fleitz Group was tasked with the design of the new space which occupies six floors in a seven-story 1970s building.

An additional goal of the relocation was to transform the operations and communications structures within the company. Two components were vital to the design: a centralized communication space to be utilized by all departments, and large, open-plan work areas to promote teamwork.

A free-floating staircase, engineered by schlaich bergermann, leads visitors to the first—and largest—floor. Here is housed the heart of the new office, a communications area consisting of the reception area, meeting spaces, dining tables, a library and conference rooms. A wide range of seating options offer just the right setting for any discussion. The company envisions this floor as a focal point for communications, not just at break times, but as an integral part of every employee's workday.

The glass facades of the individual offices are positioned differently on each floor, resulting in a varied spatial landscape. Free-floating stairs lead to the first and main floor of the six-story office.

Visitors entering the communications floor from the elevators are met with a wall inset with black magnetic strips that serve as presentation surfaces. A stripe of carpeting laid on mineral-coated concrete and a lighting strip suspended from the ceiling help to orient and guide visitors to the reception area. Behind the reception desk, below right, are desks for administrative tasks.

The five office floors above the communications floor follow a basic structure—but with some variation and much flexibility. Each houses approximately 25 workstations and a large, open-plan workspace. Work and traffic zones are separated with furniture units—all low enough for individuals to easily see over when standing, but high enough to provide privacy to those seated.

Peter Ippolito at Ippolito Fleitz sums up the project, "The new office building for schlaich bergermann und partner establishes a new communication culture and working environment within the company. The differentiated communication areas cater to the different demands of every type of collegial exchange and the varying layouts on the individual work floors produce diverse office environments."

A waiting area, above, is located opposite the reception desk and is backed by a free-standing glass shelving unit that displays accolades the firm has won over the years. The communication area, below, offers several setting options and is envisioned as an important part of the employees' daily experience.

In the center of the communication area is an ample dining section with two long tables and 24 chairs. A ceiling of sound-control plaster is suspended above. Next to the dining area is a line of small tables, left, that offer a place for more intimate conversation. The neon green dots on the floor are designed to conjure the association of a meadow, forming a conceptional bridge to a terrace located beyond the windows.

Seating options in the communication space range from the formal to the cozy and casual. A square conference table is clearly circumscribed by a dropped light field on the ceiling and a transparent latticework curtain, suggesting a semi-private space. In the library nook are two angular wingback chairs, while another seating option is enclosed in an upholstered semi-circle. Punches of bright colors add energy and appeal.

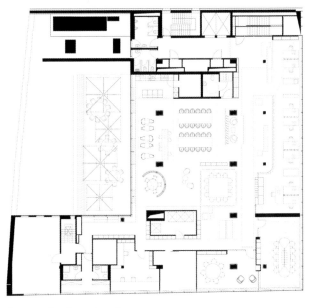

Communications level.

Two conference rooms are located on the communications floor. Both have deep-pile carpeting, silver curtains and metallic wall units to create a concentrated work ambience. In the larger of the two rooms, above, the legs of the table are a deliberately ironic play on a space frame, a reference to the firm's core area of expertise.

The five floors above the communications floor also work to improve teamwork and cooperation. A metal grid ceiling designates the movement zones of the floors and adds dynamics to the spatial axis.

Cruciform furniture units provide storage and presentation space thanks to magnetic surfaces. Structural pillars, two rows of four each, are integrated into the furniture.

DESIGN: **Ippolito Fleitz Group,** Stuttgart, Germany
CLIENT: **schlaich bergermann und partner GmbH,** Stuttgart, Germany
DESIGN TEAM: **Peter Ippolito, Gunter Fleitz, Tilla Goldberg, Christian Kirschenmann Jakub Pakula, Stefanie Maurer, Sherief Sabet, Markus Schmidt, Daniela Schröder**
PHOTOGRAPHY: **Zooey Braun**

Sharp Electronics Europe

Cornella, Spain

GRUP IDEA, Barcelona, Spain

Recently Sharp Electronics Europe developed a new Pan European-based model for its European operations, which had been country-based. An important component of Sharp's new structure is the "Centre of Excellence" that recently opened near Barcelona. The intention of Sharp with this new facility is to strengthen its European Consumer Electronics division through integrated activities such as the planning and end-to-end development of products.

The concept for the new office is far removed from the factory-orientated philosophy which Sharp followed for many years in Spain, and instead focuses on knowledge-based business tasks and R&D. Almost 100 people are employed in the new venue and the office is designed to easily accommodate more people in the future. GRUP IDEA— a company based in Barcelona and specializing in office architecture and design—was commissioned for the complete architectural design, interior decoration and construction management. The top management at Sharp called for the new venue "to feel modern, peaceful and respectful of open spaces; to promote the relationship between employees, departments and work."

The new center is located inside the World Trade Center

The product showroom, above, visible from the street, features furniture designed by GRUP IDEA specifically for each products. Every aspect of the new building is utilized to brand the company, including the entry area, below, which includes a video wall. The Sharp logo and inspirational messages can be seen throughout.

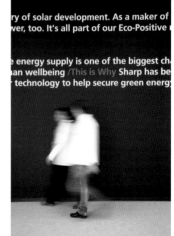

An open area of the new Sharp facility offers nature light and wide vistas.

of Almeda Park Cornella, Barcelona, a modern business park with easy access to the airport, to the rest of Europe and the world. The facility also incorporates the latest conference system technology to ensure clear communication between worldwide subsidiaries.

One requirement for the new facility, and perhaps the most important, is to promote teamwork. Sharing, cooperating and exchanging ideas are crucial to the new office's emphasis on innovation and design. With this in mind, the designers looked to the idea of an agora—the public open spaces in ancient Greece used for assembles and markets—for inspiration.

The design centers round a large, central courtyard. From this open space natural light flows directly into surrounding area, which represents the agora—the public area of the building. Here is located ample space for employees to relax and meet informally. Although distinct locations are assigned for research, administration and commercial areas within the floor plan, the open design allows for easy communication and strengthens inter-departmental relations. Only the most senior staff members have private, closed offices.

After studying the corporate identity manual, a color code was applied to walls, floors, partitions, and also to the graphics. Sharp's signature red color is found as highlights throughout the building and contrasts with the black, white and neutral graduations of grey. Various colors of vinyl

flooring are utilized to identify the different departments and many walls are painted with solid colors and inscribed with messages that encourage creativity. Instead of attempting to hide the many support pillars visible in the open space, the designer gave them a playful role by painting them with varying linear patterns in the corporate colors.

The new building does have a public face. Both the reception area and a product showroom clearly define the Sharp brand and its products to anyone visiting. Dominating the entry or reception area is a video wall displaying the company's 100 years of history and a range of products. Also in this area are chairs and tables that can serve as a waiting area for visitors or a casual meeting place for employees.

A product showroom, situated in an area of the building open to the public, displays an extensive range of Sharp's newest consumer electronic, documents and visual solution products. GRUP IDEA designed furniture specifically for each product, ensuring each item is displayed to its fullest advantage. The showroom area faces the public area of the business center, with large, clearly visible windows, offering an invitation to the public. The entire showroom and the office itself, effective convey Sharp's brand message and its one-hundred-year history of innovative products to visitors and employees alike.

Multiple departments share the large open spaces, encouraging better interdepartmental communication. Engineering and R&D areas, below, are located around a large red box with the company signature red color and messaging.

Open work areas and color-striped columns lead to the meeting rooms and closed offices that are unified near the ceiling with black-painted plasterboard.

The new Sharp facility mixes open work areas and meeting rooms. The building is situated around a central courtyard which allows large amounts of natural light to flood the space and provides a relaxing place for employees to meet.

The transparent offices allow privacy while maintaining a feeling of openness. Messaging dominates many walls.

DESIGN: **GRUP IDEA, Barcelona, Spain (www.grupidea.com)**
GRUP IDEA DESIGN TEAM: **Rodolfo Perez Martos, Alejandro Mora, Miquel Àngel Julià, Monica Morales, Ivan Gas, Roger Lopez**
CLIENT: **Sharp Electronics Europe**
PHOTOGRAPHY: **STARP ESTUDI (www.starpestudi.com)**

Snagajob.com
Richmond, VA

Baskervill, Richmond, VA

Snagajob is a company whose business is the hourly worker.

Snagajob is committed to people: the hourly worker, the companies that seek the worker, and the community at large. They love what they do and how they build a team—internally and externally. Passion and creativity were the driving forces behind the redesign of the company's new, decidedly non-corporate, corporate headquarters.

Even before the redesign, Snagajob was ranked number one in the 2011 Great Places to Work, Best Small & Medium Workplaces. They needed a physical space for up to 400 employees that would support their identity and raise it to a new level. They asked the designers at Baskervill to design a space to enhance and encourage the employee-centered company culture.

"This redesigned 68,000 sq. ft. space is a reflection of the lively culture, creativity, and camaraderie of its employees and reflects a company mentality of unapologetic passion for people—the staff, the hourly worker, and the companies they serve," states Susan Orange, Baskervill's director of workplace strategies. "It features unique design details and custom fixtures that make coming to work an enjoyable experience."

The design goals focused on several main ideas: bringing the outdoors indoors, making it fun and flexible, and encouraging teamwork and collaboration. Floor-to-ceiling windows let in light and frame views of a scenic pond right outside the windows. Fun, in an extreme sense, comes in the form of a huge aluminum slide placed in the lobby. Employees can enjoy a few playful moments and actually use it to quickly travel between the office's two floors.

To encourage collaboration, the open-plan space features areas designed to create opportunities for "casual collisions" and the exchange of ideas. There are no private offices, but an abundance of meeting spaces, both open and closed. Sense of community is reinforced at the gathering spots, including a "town center," kitchen, beer taps and most unusual, "The Hill." This is a five-tier riser that provides an engaging place for the entire company to meet, share information and celebrate what Snagajob calls "shout outs," where employees and leadership recognize outstanding performance and celebrate important business and personal milestones.

The open plan did have its challenges. Wall space was at a premium and each wall had to be carefully considered for functionality. The ceiling was designed to add height, light, details and articulation from above.

"The response from employees and leadership has been overwhelmingly positive," reports Orange. "Employees can even be seen on the weekends enjoying the space and playing ping pong, not necessarily working. The new space reinforces the client's motto 'bust it while having fun' and serves as a physical communicator of this company's culture, brand, process, and mission." Snagajob's new workspace is both functional—and cool!

The Hill is a tiered structure that provides an interesting place for employees to relax and interact.

The fun and non-corporate attitude at Snagajob is introduced in the lobby. Included are bright colors, natural light and a usable slide.

Snagajob's new office reflects the passion and creativity of the company and its employees. A cloud-filled conference room, below, provides privacy without isolation.

The slide is constantly used by employees to get from the upper level to the lower.

The kitchen provides another option for colleagues to meet in a relaxing environment.

DESIGN: **Baskervill**, Richmond, VA
DESIGNER: **Susan Orange, CID, project manager**
CLIENT: **Snagajob.com**
CONTRACTOR: **Highwoods Properties**
LIGHTING: **Diana Ades**
PHOTOGRAPHY: **Chris Cunningham**

Sportlife

Nueva Las Condes Building, Santiago, Chile

Droguett A&A Ltda., Santiago, Chile

Sportlife is a modern chain of fitness centers in Chile dedicated to making a positive impact on the quality of life for people of all ages and abilities. Since its founding it has remained focused on strengthening the health and welfare of the communities it serves.

Droguett A&A of Santiago was recently charged with the design of new, 4,941 sq. ft. corporate offices for Sportlife. Important to the company, and a challenge to the designers, was the creation of a space that would reflect the fitness chain's vision of modernity and wellbeing. Needed was a design that would incorporate elements from the brand's fitness centers and philosophy into the workplace environment.

The energy, activity and movement inherent in a gym is captured in the office's basic layout. A wide sweeping corridor begins at the reception desk and forms a track of sorts through almost the entire office, curving at each end. To the inner side of the corridor are located open work areas with half-height partitions. To the outside are private and semi-private offices and meeting rooms. The corridor is defined with a ceiling of dark wood beams, placed dynamically from side to side and furthering the sense of movement.

Floor-to-ceiling sandblasted glass partitions line the corridor and give privacy to the outer offices and meeting rooms while still allowing natural light to reach the inner workstations. The partitions also give a contemporary look to the interior.

The designers approached the materials selection by relating the working areas of the office with the workout areas of a gym, and the common spaces of the office to relaxation areas in a gym. Warm, natural wood veneers cover the walls of the office's common areas and contrast with the white walls of the work areas. And, in what has to be one of the most inventive and employee-friendly ideas for the workplace, the vinyl flooring used in the offices is the same as that used in professional exercise rooms—durable and very easy on the feet.

The main corridor has a ceiling with dark wood beams, while over the work area is a visible concrete slab that sets that area apart.

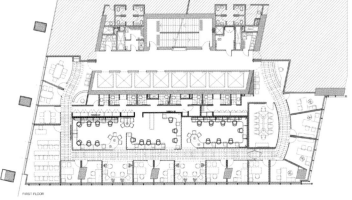

FIRST FLOOR

The design artfully balances the warm aesthetic of the common areas with contemporary work areas. Elements from the company's fitness centers are also used in the office. For instance, vinyl flooring in the offices is the same as is found on the floors of high-tech exercise rooms. Approximately 50 people work in the new office.

Floor-to-ceiling sandblasted glass partitions line the corridor.

DESIGN: **Droguett A&A Ltda.,** Santiago, Chile
ARCHITECT, DIRECTOR: **Freddy Droguett H.**
ARCHITECT, PROJECT DESIGNERS: **Maria Antonieta Cepeda, Francisco Tobar**
CLIENT: **Sportlife**
CONTRACTOR: **Andrés Link, Constructora LNK**
FURNITURE AND WORKSTATION DESIGN: **Fernando Mayer**
PHOTOGRAPHY: **Marcos Medizabal**

THQ Studio
Montreal, QC, Canada

id+s Design Solutions, Montreal, QC, Canada

The screening room features an innovative revolving door and theatrical seating.

Montreal design firm id+s Design Solutions was commissioned to design the office of THQ, an American developer and publisher of video games. Located in an historic building, the former headquarters and printing facilities of the Montreal Gazette newspaper, THQ's largest development studio in Montreal now occupies the 57,000 sq. ft. space on two floors.

This massive studio with a 400–person capacity includes a wide spectrum of disciplines that serve as THQ's creative engine. The client's objective was to maximize the number of people in a collaborative workplace setting and social zones while maintaining close interaction and optimize communication between the various work departments.

The large floor plates were divided into two distinctive zones: a darker atmosphere was designated for the artists, a brighter outdoor setting in honeycomb-shaped workstations and wooden "skate park" platforms, for the other disciplines. Over-sized metal poles, feed the electrical and communication cabling, and create an abstraction of trees or lampposts. Connecting these two zones is a giant-sized white tunnel incorporating social gathering spaces and offices.

Complementary rooms took on various themes and purposes, becoming multifunctional. The lunchroom turns into an outdoor rest stop; the screening room exposes its theatrical side, and conference room tables transform into ping-pong tables.

Each zone plays out as a series of screen shots underscoring the culture of the multi-media industry, work at play, and emulates the very nature of the organization.

The colorful lunchroom is a collective social zone for gathering and relaxation.

Connecting the two zones—artists in one and the other disciplines in the another—is a giant-sized white tunnel incorporating social gathering spaces and offices.

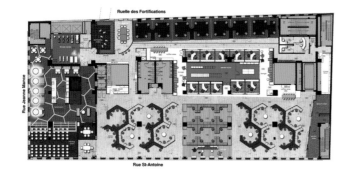

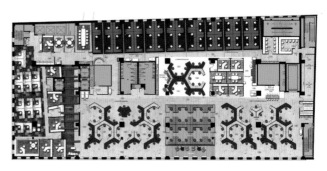

A darker atmosphere was designated for the artists, left, and a brighter outdoor setting for the other disciplines.

197

An open work area has honeycomb-shaped workstations and wooden "skate park" platforms.

Spaces take on dual purposes, becoming multifunctional—a hallway becomes a casual meeting area and a conference room tables transform into ping-pong tables. Even heating up lunch takes place in a fun environment, below.

DESIGN: **id+s Design Solutions Inc.**, Montreal, QC, Canada
PROJECT LEADER: **Susie Silveri**
DESIGN TEAM: **Stefania Pasto, Pascale Fouchard**
CLIENT: **THQ Studio**
ARCHITECT: **Réal Paul**
ENGINEERS: **Bouthillette Parizeau**
PHOTOGRAPHY: **Claude-Simon Langlois**

Tribal DDB Amsterdam

Amsterdam, The Netherlands

i29 interior architects, Amsterdam, The Netherlands

Tribal DDB Amsterdam is a digital marketing agency and part of DDB International, a large international advertising network. Recently the Amsterdam-based firm, i29 interior architects, was tasked with the design of Tribal DDB's new office for approximately 80 people.

At the core of the design directive were several contradictions. Needed was an environment that would support creative interaction among employees and allow for as many workstations as possible within a large, open space. However, the need for individual focus could not be sacrificed. Jasper Jansen of i29 continues the explanation, "Also, as Tribal DDB is part of an international network, a clear identity was required which would fit the parent company. The design had to reflect an identity that is friendly and playful, but also professional and serious. The contradictions within these requirements called for choices that would allow for great flexibility in the design."

Adding to the challenge were unmovable structural elements that had to be integrated into the design and the problematic acoustics of the large space, a real problem in an office meant for both collaboration and concentration.

The designers searched for one grand gesture that could address all of these challenges. They began by selecting a felted fabric to serve as both a ceiling system and to cover the hindering structural elements. This choice led to the realization that the material could solve many of their other problems as well. Felt, a nonwoven fabric that is produced by condensing and pressing woolen fibers, can take on many tasks and characters—both playful and powerful. It is perfect for absorbing sound and creates warmth and privacy in large open spaces. Other advantages include being durable, fireproof and environmentally friendly. After deciding upon felt, the designers placed it everywhere—on floors, ceiling, walls, furniture and lampshades. "This doesn't mean it was easy to make all of these items in one material," says Jansen.

The resulting modern, light-filled office fulfills its mission—encouraging interaction and providing quiet places to work. It's welcoming, warm and professional.

Jansen concludes, "We all know how hard it is to stay focused on the one thing that is most important to us. It is the same way with design. The result of being very selective is that you have to push the one choice to the limit. It also provides a field of tension, and gives energy to a space without falling into chaos. But more importantly, it leaves you with a charismatic environment."

While the office is an open space, dividers afford privacy and wool felt, the material used on many surfaces, quiets the space and unifies the light-filled room.

Various shades of gray and distinctive shapes are seen throughout the office. Even the paired lampshades gently contrast one another.

DESIGN: **i29 interior architects**, Amsterdam, The Netherlands
CONTRACTOR: **Slavenburg**
CLIENT: **Tribal DDB Amsterdam,** Amsterdam, The Netherlands
PHOTOGRAPHY: **i29 interior architects**

venturethree

London, UK

Brinkworth, London, UK

Venturethree, a brand identity consultancy located in Mayfair, London, recently found themselves in need of additional office space. They had previously worked with Brinkworth, a London design firm, to transform what were second-floor squash courts into a flexible, contemporary studio. Now they again turned to Brinkworth to renovate the ground-floor garage space directly underneath into the needed additional offices. Important to the client and designers was that continuity between the two floors be established and the contemporary atmosphere already in place be maintained.

Kevin Brennan of Brinkworth says, "The challenge was to rival the spatial quality of the top space. The upper floor's indulgent height could never be matched, but the transparent elevation onto the courtyard compensates for the lost vertical height. The lack of decorative accessories in the first scheme made it a pleasure to revisit the design if only to confirm the client and our team had it right the first time."

The relationship between the two floors is established and enhanced by the extension of vertical planes. An interior wall made of pegboard runs the full height of the building, cutting through the floor and creating a physical manifestation of the desired unity between levels. The green-painted, innovative material is multi-functional; it serves as a handy place to mount presentation boards and it helps correct the intrusive acoustics of the former squash court.

Also running the full height of the space is a bright red wall introduced in the open stairwell. The striking red color was used elsewhere to add contrast to the otherwise neutral color palette. In a new meeting room both the laminate tabletop and the upholstery of the Eames Soft Pad chairs sport the bright color.

Tanya Redgrave of venturethree says, "Our fantastic new studio space gives us flexibility, as well as a light and open environment to work in a truly collaborative way. We're in the business of creating world-class brands and now we have a world-class space in which to do this."

Glass replaces garage doors on the ground floor of the facade, compensating for the lack of vertical height and opening the space to the exterior. The renovation maintains the open plan and contemporary atmosphere created by Brinkworth for the original studio.

The unity between the floors is enhanced by the bright red stairwell wall and the industrial Croughtrie lamps that drop almost 23 feet, connecting the large open space.

To create consistency with the original studio, Brinkworth utilized the same materials as before, including the raw, English oak flooring. The designers also created luminous desktops which, after the lights go off, glow futuristically in the dark.

Seating units include built-in cupboards with sliding doors—creating easily accessed storage units and much flexibility. Seamless glass walls give privacy to the new meeting rooms, below, while maintaining the feeling of open space.

DESIGN: **Brinkworth**, London, UK
CLIENT: **venturethree**
PHOTOGRAPHY: **Paul Tyagi, Lara Gosling & Louise Melchior**

voestalpine Stahl GmbH

Linz, Austria

Dietmar Feichtinger Architectes, Paris, France

Following a competition between several top-rank design-ers, Dietmar Feichtinger Architectes was chosen to design the new Linz headquarters of Voestalpine Stahl GmbH in an expansive open area. The dynamically curved building, cut at an angle in front, with the filigree and adjustable golden façade unfailingly draws the attention of passing traffic.

To create a representative whole, the designers config-ured a plan that combined three very different buildings and united the wasteland area to the north of the company headquarters to the visitor's center in the south via a clearly bordered open space. The resultant two-level park is set to become one of the city's most prominent parks.

Underground parking consisting of reinforced concrete, planted embankments, natural cross-ventilation, and light-ing from planted atria keeps the site clear of vehicles. At the main entrance to the sales and finance office is a daring cantilever exploiting steel's structural possibilities. The com-pany's primary product, steel, is also highlighted at the steel reception desk.

From reception an elevator takes the visitors to the meet-ing rooms. The top floor is open to the sky and a terrace with glass walls offers exceptional views of the surrounding area.

The dynamically curved building, cut at an angle in front, unfailingly draws attention.

On the ground floor behind a delicately profiled glass façade are rooms for the company travel agency, archive, advertising media department, and more.

A shimmering golden façade encases the main offices on the four upper floors. The offices are designed in a double-loaded linear fashion. However, the curve of the building visually reduces the apparent length. Four glass-roofed atria are situated in a center zone along which the offices lie. Beside each atrium is located a "living room" to ease circulation and employee interaction. The offices are separated from these areas by glass walls. The interior's color scheme has gentle shades of grey complemented by the light brown of the wooden floors as well as the brighter shades in the area of the tea kitchens.

On the façade, sliding shade elements of frameless expanded metal on the outside, and the textile glare protection on the inside ensure agreeable lighting conditions. The building services can be made out behind their expanded metal cladding above the corridors. The discipline that this demanded in both design and execution adds a further level of quiet elegance to the overall impression.

The company's primary product, steel, is highlighted at the steel reception desk. On the ground floor are rooms for the company travel agency, archive, advertising media department, and more.

One of building's four
glass-roofed atria.

Beside each atrium is located a "living room" to ease circulation and employee interaction, this page and opposite. The offices are separated from these areas by glass walls which curve to visually reduce the building's apparent length. The interior's color scheme has gentle shades of grey complemented by the light brown of the wooden floors as well as the brighter shades in the area of the tea kitchens.

The offices on the four upper floors are ensured agreeable lighting conditions by the facade's sliding shade elements and the textile glare protection on the inside.

The top floor is open to the sky and a terrace with glass walls offers exceptional views of the surrounding area.

DESIGN: **Dietmar Feichtinger Architectes**, Paris, France
PROJECT TEAM LEADERS: **Claire Bodénez, Gerhard Pfeiler**
TEAM: **Philipp Hugo Urabl, Dorit Böhme, Roland Basista, Albert Moosbrugger,**
Ulli Gabriel, Andreas Trampe-Kieslich, Ralitsa Kafova, Camille Duperche,
Katharina Düsing, Nemanja Kordic
CLIENT: **voestalpine Stahl GmbH**
ENGINEERS: **Schindelar ZT_GmbH**
ENGINEERS, ROOF STRUCTURE: **Werkraum ZT GmbH**
PHOTOGRAPHY: **Jo Feichtinger, Josef Pausch, Barbara_Feichtinger-Felber**

Woodward Design+Build

New Orleans, LA

Commercial Design Interiors, LLC, Baton Rouge, LA
Woodward Design+Build, New Orleans, LA

When Woodward Design+Build recently moved out of their old facility and around the corner into a brand new building—both locations in the Central City neighborhood of New Orleans—it was an opportunity for the company to put into practice what it has long preached: sustainable design.

As a firm dedicated to sustainable design and building techniques, the new headquarters had to uphold and showcase these practices. "Everyone involved in the development, from Woodward Design+Build's internal project team and architects, the interior designers from Commercial Design Interiors, LLC, and various consultants, handled it as a full dress rehearsal for the future of the construction and sustainable design industry," explains Matthew Edmonds co-owner of Commercial Design Interiors.

The project is on a LEED certification track due to the team's careful site selection and building orientation, the use of high efficiency lighting and renewable energy—solar panels sit on the roof—and sustainable interior design practices. Materials with recycled and renewable content were sourced and efficient, resource-conserving mechanical, electrical and plumbing systems utilized.

The solar panels, 277 in number, supply the building's energy needs and is currently working 23% above the rate of capacity. Also gracing the roof are low maintenance plantings, a huge advantage in the New Orleans sunshine over traditional, heat-absorbing materials. The roof garden also reduces storm water run-off and provides employees with outdoor seating and spectacular views of the city.

Woodward believes that its employees are what makes the company strong and successful, therefore they were given a strong voice in the development of the form and functionality of the building. Designers consulted with each area of the company that will use the new building and worked that feedback into the finished design. The result is a employee-friendly workplace. There's an abundance of natural light, a rooftop patio for relaxation, and plenty of space for meetings, impromptu collaborations and special events. In an effort to bring new business into the neighborhood, ground floor retail space is included in the design.

The office follows an open plan with private offices located away from the perimeter, leaving the large windows and natural light to the workstations—which are kept low to increase the daylighting and views.

If all of this is not enough, the design of the new Woodward headquarters also effectively brands the company, helping to shape public and client opinion of the firm. When guests enter from the ground floor level they are met with marketing elements and core value statements and prompted with wayfinding signage to proceed up the monumental stairs or the elevator to the reception area on the second level. This main reception area is an expression of the Woodward brand. The desk's design and finishes all conceptually showcase Woodward's core businesses: Design Group, Steel Group, Millwork Group, Engineering Group and Service Group. Throughout the building the use of materials—glass wood, steel and aluminum—along with the company's logo and signage, communicate the company's capabilities and sustainable ethics.

Woodward Design+Build traces its New Orleans roots to 1923 and their new headquarters is still located in the center of the city. The building reflects the spirit of innovation that defines Woodward's approach to business. A staircase, visible from the outside, extends from the ground floor to the third level. Its open surroundings provide ease of communication between floors.

When guests enter on the ground level they are prompted with wayfinding signage to proceed to the reception area on the second level. The reception desk, designed by Commercial Design Interiors, uses a wide palette of materials and finishes to showcase Woodward's many capabilities. The Woodward logo visually anchors the desk to the space.

Open workstations are located around the perimeter of the building, taking advantage of the abundant daylight. A detail of the reception desk illustrates the designer's use of glass, wood, steel and aluminium and juxtaposes delicate and rigid properties of the materials.

The vegetated roof garden provides employees with outdoor seating while helping to keep the building cool and reducing storm water run-off. Solar panels supply the building's energy needs and is currently working 23% above the rate of capacity. The 235-watt panels make up a 65 kilowatt system.

Collaboration is at the heart of Woodward's business model and having enough meeting spaces to accommodate the needs of its 270 employees was a major concern. The building features six formal meeting rooms with varying capacities and numerous smaller spaces for impromptu meetings. Wayfinding signage is used as an opportunity to strengthen the Woodward brand.

DESIGN: **Matthew Edmonds, Tracy Burns, Commercial Design Interiors, LLC,** Baton Rouge, LA
PROJECT ARCHITECT: **Erik Wismar, Woodard Design+Build,** New Orleans, LA
CLIENT: **Woodward Design+Build,** New Orleans, LA
MARKETING: **Robert Norton, Woodward Design+Build; Zande+Newman Design**
PHOTOGRAPHY: **Jeff Johnston, Jeff Johnston Photography; Matthew Edmonds,
Commercial Design Interiors, LLC**

INDEX OF DESIGNERS/ARCHITECTS

Dietmar Feichtinger Architectes
 VOESTALPINE STAHL GMBH, 208
11, Rue des Vignoles
75020 Paris, France
Phone: 33-01-43-71-1522
Fax: 33-01-43-70-67-20
Email: contact.paris@feichtingerarchitectes.com
www.feichtingerarchitectes.com

Droguett A&A Ltda.
 SPORTLIFE, 190
Padre Mariano #10.
Ofic. 306 –- Providencia
Santiago, Chile
Phone: 562-235-5567
Fax: 562-235-1753
www.daa.cl

Grup Idea
 SHARP ELECTRONICS EUROPE, 180
Plaça de l'Angel 2, 2n 1a.
08002 Barcelona, Spain
Phone: 34-902-021-707
grupidea@grupidea.com
www.grupidea.com

Hérault Arnod Architectes
 ROSSIGNOL, 162
16, rue Thiers
38 000 Grenoble, France
Phone: 33-04-76-12-94-94
Fax: 33-04-76-86-11-44
Email: zzz@herault-arnod.fr
www.herault-arnod.fr

i29 interior architects
 GUMMO, 74
 OFFICE HERENGRACHT, 148
 TRIBAL DDB AMSTERDAM, 200
Industrieweg 29
1115 AD Duivendrecht
The Netherlands
Phone: 31-20-695-61-20
Email: info@i29.nl
www.i29.nl

id+s Design Solutions
 THQ STUDIO, 194
486 Ste-Catherine West, Suite 410
Montreal, QC H3B 1A6
Phone: 514-390-0003
Fax: 514-393-9006
Email: info@ids-design.com
www.ids-design.com

Ippolito Fleitz Group
 SCHLAICH BERGERMANN UND PARTNER, 172
Augustenstrasse 87
70197 Stuttgart, Germany
Phone: 49-0711-993392-330
Fax: 49-0711-993392-333
Email: info@ifgroup.org
www.ifgroup.org

IwamotoScott Architecture
 OBSCURA DIGITAL, 142
729 Tennessee Street
San Francisco, CA 94107
Phone: 415-864-2868
Email: contact@iwamotoscott.com
www.iwamotoscott.com

JPC Architects
 JPC ARCHITECTS, 110
909 112th Ave NE Suite 206
Bellevue, WA 98004
Phone: 425-641-9200
Fax: 425-637-8200
www.jpcarchitects.com

Lemay associés [architecture, design]
 ASTRAL MEDIA, 34
780, Av. Brewster, 4e étage
Montreal, QC, Canada H4C 2K1
Phone: 514-932-5101
Fax: 514 935-8137
www.lemay.qc.ca

Mancini•Duffy/TSC
 AOL, 26
275 Seventh Avenue, 19th Floor
New York, NY 10001
Phone: 212-938-1260
Email: bsotomayor@manciniduffy.com
www.manciniduffy.com

MAS · ARQUITECTURA
 LOSAN GROUP, 124
 MNPROGRAM, 134
San Andrés 67
15003 A Coruña
Phone: 981-202-716
Fax: 881-926-251
www.mas.es

Michael Malone Architects, Inc.
HEWLETT PACKARD (HP), 78
HIGHLAND CAPITAL MANAGEMENT, 84
INTERCERAMIC, 102
JENTERRA, 106
5646 Milton Street, Suite 705
Dallas, TX 75206
Phone: 214-969-5440
www.mma2000.com

Ministry of Design
LEO BURNETT OFFICE, 120
20 Cross Street #03-01 Singapore 048422
Phone: 65-6222-5780
Email: studio@modonline.com
http://www.modonline.com

NFOE et associés architectes
BUREAU 100, 50
511 Place d'Armes, bureau 100
Montréal, QC, H2Y 2W7
Phone: 514-397-2616
Fax: 514-861-5242
Email: info@nfoe.com
www.nfoe.com

OTJ Architects
NATIONAL PARKS CONSERVATION
ASSOCIATION, 138
1412 Eye Street, NW
(Zei Alley Entrance)
Washington, DC 20005
Phone: 202-621-1000
Fax: 202-621-1001
Email: marshall@otj.com
http://www.otj.com

plajer & franz studio
PLAJER & FRANZ STUDIO, 154
erkelenzdamm 59/61
10999 Berlin, Germany
Phone: 49-030-616-5580
Fax: 49-030-616-55819
Email: studio@plajer-franz.de
www.plajer-franz.de

Spector Group
ACOTEL GROUP, 10
FOREST SOLUTIONS GROUP, 70
MASON CAPITAL MANAGEMENT, 132
183 Madison Avenue
New York New York 10016
Phone: 212-599-0055
Fax: 212-599-1043
Email: sespector@spectorgroup.com
www.spectorgroup.com

Stiff + Trevillion Architects
INNOCENT, 96
16 Woodfield Road
London, W9 2BE UK
Phone: 44-020-8960-5550
Fax: 44-020-8969-8668
Email: mail@stiffandtrevillion.com
www.stiffandtrevillion.com

Tobin | Parnes Design
ACTIV FINANCIAL, 14
304 Hudson Street, Suite 500
New York, NY 10013-1015
Phone: 212-462-4200
Fax: 212-462-4788
Email: tpde@tobinparnes.com
www.tobinparnes.com

Woodward Design+Build
WOODWARD DESIGN+BUILD, 216
1000 South Jefferson Davis Parkway
New Orleans, LA 70125
Phone: 504-822-6443
Fax: 504-822-9493
www.woodwarddesignbuild.com

Yost Grube Hall Architecture
ATER WYNNE, 40
M FINANCIAL GROUP, 128
1211 SW 5th Avenue, Suite 2700
Portland, OR 97204 USA
Phone: 503-221-0150
Email: info@ygh.com
www.ygh.com